MILLARD SHEETS ·

ONE-MAN RENAISSANCE

WATERMELON LADY *watercolor* *22 x 30 inches* *1983*

·MILLARD · SHEETS·
ONE-MAN RENAISSANCE

by JANICE LOVOOS and EDMUND F. PENNEY
Foreword by RICHARD ARMOUR

NORTHLAND PRESS FLAGSTAFF, ARIZONA

CONTENTS

FOREWORD

The descriptive title of this revealing and fascinating biography is well chosen. Had it been "Renaissance Man," it would have suggested the quality of its subject, but at first glance it might have led some to believe that Millard Sheets was a contemporary of Leonardo da Vinci, the fifteenth-century master.

Fortunately for those of us who have had the privilege of knowing Millard, his birth occurred considerably later than the fifteenth or even the sixteenth century, when Renaissance art flourished. In fact, I was born a year before Millard, although it is only in my birthdate that I admit to being a little ahead of him.

"One-Man Renaissance" is a good description of Millard. At a time when there are not many figures of renaissance quality, except perhaps in science, Millard is a renaissance unto himself. Instead of being a great artist in a time of great artists, a time of "flowering of the human spirit," Millard epitomizes artistic rebirth.

For many years I have had another word for Millard. I have called him a genius, and I use the word sparingly. In my lifetime I have known only four persons toward whom the word "genius" applies. (For a while I told people I have known five, but a few years ago I dropped one from my list.) Millard has been on my list the longest, and is in no danger of being dropped. His place is secure.

The qualities of a genius are, I think, the following: early manifestation of talent, unstoppable drive, and the ability to soar to the heights of achievement in a wide variety of fields. That these qualities are present in the life and accomplishments of Millard Sheets will be readily apparent to any reader of this biography.

Though I have known Millard almost all my life, I knew him best when we were fellow members of the faculty at Scripps College. He may be most widely known for his paintings, murals, architectural designs, and on and on, but I knew him as an extraordinary college professor. Somehow he managed to bring to a small college a distinguished group of painters, sculptors, and ceramists to work with him. Meanwhile, he inspired many students not merely to pass courses in art but to become creative artists themselves.

On the personal side, as well as front and back, I am most impressed by his warm personality, his bear-hug way of greeting a friend, his frankness in expressing an opinion, his vitality, and his incessant drive to do more and more, better and better. The years do not weaken him, they ripen him.

What a man! He is indeed, with Mary always his worthy, faithful helper, a one-man renaissance.

RICHARD ARMOUR

INTRODUCTION

CANNOT RECALL THE EXACT CIRCUMSTANCES which led to a first encounter with Millard Sheets, but it was inevitable that one day we would meet. For we were part of a group of artist-students who lived in a creative milieu that was just beginning to find its voice in the Los Angeles of the twenties. We all knew one another, or at least knew about one another. Everybody knew about Millard Sheets.

It was a fortunate time and place to be coming of age, especially for an artist. Art in Los Angeles was as young and naive as we were. There was a prevailing camaraderie in those less self-conscious, friendlier times, which are not likely to recur in the overpopulated, traffic-burdened, not-so-innocent city it has become.

Long before freeways, years before smog, California was blessed with a voluptuous, natural kind of beauty that artists find irresistible. A vast blue ocean stretched for miles, hugging a romantic coastline. Meadows billowed with lupin and golden poppies.

It was a travel folder come to life—Paradise found—and it all belonged to the artist.

On weekends, with sketch pads and easels, artists dotted the seashore, the harbors, the verdant slopes of Elysian Park, and the dry washes of the Arroyo Seco. A veritable army of painters attacked the endless stands of eucalyptus trees with brush and palette. The whole glowing landscape was there to celebrate, as close to the artist as the tip of a brush.

This was the aesthetic climate in southern California when Millard Sheets burst upon the local art scene. He did not emerge gently. Gifted and gutsy, disarming and dynamic, he possessed a vitality that made waves whenever he appeared.

Dalzell Hatfield, foremost West Coast art dealer of that period, was quick to realize the young man's potential; Hatfield added Sheets's name to a roster of established artists. What a team they made: Sheets with his considerable talent and youthful enthusiasm, Hatfield with his expertise and a powerful gift of persuasion. Before long, Sheets's paintings had found permanent homes in museums and collections as famous as those of Ruth Maitland and the discerning Wright Ludington of Santa Barbara. As one of his peers, I was aware, as we all were, that this young man was different. Unique and dedicated, he seemed earmarked for success.

The year 1929 was important in shaping Millard's professional career as an artist. After graduating from Chouinard's School of Art, his first major one-man show was presented by Ruth and Dalzell Hatfield in their gallery. Before that auspicious event, however, he received a telegram announcing that he had won second place in the annual Edgar B. Davis competition held in San Antonio, Texas: the award was a $1,750 cash prize. Imagine how vast that sum must have looked to a very young man just out of art school, and how his head must have been bursting with ideas as to how he would spend it.

It enabled him to travel, first to New York, then to Paris, the *pièce de résistance,* the place that all artists longed to visit. Millard's arrival in Paris was an eye-opener, and his introduction to a foreign culture stimulated a built-in avidity for learning.

His youth, ambition, and winning ways made a deep impression on Dorfinant, the master printer of Paris, who quickly made a place for this creative fledgling in his busy studio. Thus, Sheets was able to be part of a workshop that included Henri Matisse and others as well as gifted young art students, all involved in producing lithographs.

Despite the glamour, fun, and excitement of the trip, Millard was in a hurry to get back to America and sink some roots. The truth was, Millard had fallen in love. Shortly before he left for Europe, he had met Mary Baskerville, a student at the University of California at Los Angeles.

With his usual passionate pursuit of anything that moved him deeply—and Mary had—he swept her completely off her feet, and after a whirlwind two-week courtship, they were engaged. She promised to marry him on his return to the States. His prize money was depleted when he headed for home. They were married five months later, and within a year they had established a home, and their first child, Millard Owen Sheets, was born.

By 1935, New Yorkers had their first glimpse of Sheets's paintings. Compared to the relatively grey landscape of the East Coast, the freedom of expression in both oil and watercolor of his California scenery had a freshness and vitality. National recognition by New York critics gave rise to a new wave of admiration and respect as well as comments on the inevitable fading of what they termed his Johnny-come-lately talent.

Sheets was always able to artfully dodge the arrows of his critics' bows. He was willing to listen to men of broader knowledge and experience. He had the humility and the business acumen to bend his talents in any direction that might prove valuable. He never lived in an ivory tower. If one door closed, another seemed ready to open, and Sheets took advantage of every opportunity to investigate. He began to spread his creative wings as both a designer and a teacher. His horizons broadened.

Between those years and the present lie vast stretches of industry and accomplishment. Today, Millard Sheets is generally recognized as a most gifted, innovative, and resourceful artist. His fame has expanded to international prominence as artist, architectural designer and consultant, educator, lecturer, and diplomat. His enormous body of work includes paintings in all mediums, mosaics, frescoes, and mural paintings. Buildings he has designed may be seen throughout the United States. He has touched the hearts and the minds of people of such divergent tastes and cultures as Japan, New Zealand, Hawaii, Mexico, India, Egypt, and the lotus land of Hollywood. Sheets has been labeled everything from "prima donna" to "sponsoring angel," from "difficult" to "artist's best friend," from "promoter" to "genius."

There is something to be said for old acquaintances. One watches the road signs along the way, observing the events as they happen. But distance lends understanding. A kaleidoscopic view of the near-past allows one to see how the bits and pieces fit together to create the whole fabric of a full and productive life. The pattern has been there from the beginning, but only the outline was seen. Now the threads of the complex design have been woven into a tapestry of achievement, and the tapestry must be reexamined in the light of a developing perspective and rewoven into the fabric of a book.

What were the strengths that produced such an incredible career? What were the turning points? What motivated the tremendous energy to carry on such a multifaceted life, always with the enthusiasm of the nineteen-year-old boy?

There are no easy answers in trying to define the complex character of Millard Sheets, especially since the subject has been a valued friend through the years. There is a temptation to overpraise, to indulge in superlatives, to crow too loudly over the victories. To write a book of praise is not the intention of the author, and the advantage of long friendship outweighs the risk. Special, private moments, personal insights developed over a long period of time quickly reveal what months of research might fail to disclose. Just jog the memory and a bell rings. A certain image comes to mind.

"Oh, yes. I remember that. That's the way we were. That's how it really happened."

JANICE LOVOOS

An imposing sculpted sea lion stands as sentinel at Barking Rocks, home of Mary and Millard Sheets.

DEFINING MILLARD SHEETS

TRAVELING NORTH OF SAN FRANCISCO, CALIfornia, on coastal Highway One is an experience of rare beauty. The verdant, rolling hills and sleek, rounded cattle of Mendocino County are on one side, and the vastness of the Pacific Ocean is on the other. White-flecked waves roll in hypnotic repetition against sand and rock beaches, hundreds of feet below the level of the road.

Firmly anchored on a spectacular portion of this coastline, a sharp left turn off the highway, is Barking Rocks, home and haven for artist Millard Sheets and his wife, Mary. It is here that they have come to earth—a lovely part of the earth at that, wave-washed, covered by flowering vegetation, and constantly altered by the panorama of the ocean. Their home is a bi-level structure, with a wall of glass framing the sea on the west side of the lower level. A prominent feature of this area is a tripod-mounted telescope, through which one can observe hundreds of sea lions, sunning themselves on their official sanc-tuary, Fish Rock Island. The Sheetses named their home Barking Rocks in honor of the animals' hoarse cry, which can be heard round-the-clock. It is not an unpleasant sound; rather, in combination with the ocean's muted rhythm, it provides a comforting back-drop, similar to that of a ticking clock.

Even though Barking Rocks is now their only residence, as opposed to the days when they maintained a large apartment in Pasadena or a home in the Padua Hills as well, the Sheetses do not spend all their time here. Accompanied by Mary, Millard Sheets actively leads touring artists' workshops in far-flung sites around the world. They return to their home, filled with an eclectic assortment of pre-Columbian and Oriental art, sea shells, books, and comfortable furniture, to rest and prepare for their next adventure.

Millard Sheets has lived an adventurous life. Born in 1907, he has spent virtually all of his time involved in some sort of frenetic, creative activity. He is a gracious man, a warm and sharing individual who is

photograph: Leland Lee

The panorama of the Pacific Ocean and Fish Rock Island are serene backdrops for Sheets's studio, a light-filled work place.

also strong-willed, optimistic, and eager for new challenges, new experiences, and new opportunities. This combination of personality traits has served him well, enabling him to achieve major successes in a variety of endeavors. An artist, a teacher, and an entrepreneur, Sheets has always urged people to recognize the dignity of illustration and the beauty of decoration.

Inspired by the sights and colors of a recent trip into Mexico, Sheets spends hours in his studio—a light-filled, airy building separate from the house—translating his experiences into art. Watercolor, oils, and acrylics are all familiar and comfortable mediums for him. Primarily a representational painter, Sheets often uses watercolors because he values their adaptability and the ease with which they can be used and transported.

Millard Sheets grew up in California and learned to appreciate and create art in a singularly uninhibited and unstructured atmosphere. He also had a variety of inspired instructors and mentors, who supported his vision and courage to experiment. He traveled into aesthetic areas that were very lightly inhabited, and by virtue of talent and timing, established benchmarks of achievement in a variety of fields.

Vision is important to Millard Sheets—not the simple anatomical ability to perceive objects within a field of sight, but the unique inner talent to see with the heart, to capture subtle underlying voice and structure. In this respect, Sheets leans strongly toward the abstractionists, although he himself has chosen not to pursue their extremes of shape and color. He does, however, concur with the concepts they demonstrate: he teaches his students the vital lesson of defining the rhythm of shapes and color, and practices this theory himself. His work—whether in watercolor, oil, acrylic, or lithograph—is reflective of the skill with which he applies this knowledge.

The art, murals, and buildings Sheets has created during his long and productive lifetime have brought him national and international acclaim. But this present state of social and artistic recognition was not achieved overnight; it has been the culmination of a long journey. Regardless of the obstacles and hard work endured along the way, Sheets shows no sign of regret or reservation about his choices.

Sheets was able to develop his potential and take his career as far as he did by virtue of incredible self-discipline, developed and internalized during his childhood. The guiding force in his young life was his maternal grandfather, Lewis Owen. Millard's mother, the daughter of Lewis and Emma Owen, died in childbirth; shattered and grieving, his father, John Sheets, was not prepared to be both mother and provider for young Millard. He turned his infant son over to his in-laws, who still had two daughters at home. Grieved as they must have been, the arrival of a boy in the almost all-female household seemed like a miracle to Lewis Owen, and he loved his grandson fiercely. He taught Millard to appreciate all the things he himself loved, particularly horses.

Owen was physically small but very determined. Raised in Illinois, he married while still a very young man, and he and his wife moved to South Dakota to farm. Vicious winters and dry summers did their best to defeat him, but he hung on. At one point, Owen was so desperate for money that he undertook to challenge a particularly brutal fighter. The man who could stay in the ring with this accomplished pugilist would win $300, and Owen walked off with the prize.

In addition to farming, he bred and raised racehorses. His first introduction to California came when he brought some of his horses from South Dakota to the racetrack at Santa Anita. Enraptured by the climate and the many acres of orange groves, Owen moved his family to Pomona late in the nineteenth century. After some pulling up of stakes and relocating to South Dakota, they again settled, this time permanently, in California in 1897. They lived on a ranch with stables and row after row of orange trees.

It was in this environment that Millard Owen Sheets grew up. His young aunts spent hours playing with him, giving him crayons and pencils to experiment with as soon as he was able to hold them. Lewis Owen put him on his first pony at the age of three, and shortly thereafter began the child's education in the care and breeding of horses. "It's all in the dam," Sheets says today. "A good mare contributes at least 85 percent to successful offspring." This was one of the many lessons he learned from his grandfather.

Later, Millard experienced a more severe lesson when he failed to follow his grandfather's direction regarding the care and respect due the horse. Not only did Millard forget to be smarter than his mount, as Owen told him repeatedly that he must be; he also thought he could outsmart his grandfather, and found that the consequences of his misjudgment were calamitous.

In an effort to impress a little neighbor girl, the eight-year-old Millard planned to race past her gate on his flying steed. He thought his opportunity had come when, one night at the supper table, Lewis Owen announced that the next day he would not be accompanying Millard on their customary early-morning ride through the orange groves. He had an appointment in town and had to leave home at first light.

The next day, Sheets remembers, he slept rather later than usual and then saddled his mare and rode down the driveway. As he approached the gate, he began to apply the leather quirt with vigor to the horse's soft underbelly, urging her to build up speed for his dash past the girl's gate. Just as horse and rider flashed through the entrance to the drive, a hand reached out and grabbed the boy by the nape of the neck, jerking him from the mare's back.

Owen had returned early, and guessing what his grandson was up to, lay in wait for him. He was furious with the boy for what he considered poor judgment and lack of common concern for his horse. For the first and only time in his entire life, he struck Millard, sending him to the ground. The child was then peremptorily directed to go to his room and to stay there until summoned.

Both adult and child suffered that day—Owen with the fury and regret that only deep love can generate, and Millard with the knowledge that he had deeply disappointed the person who meant the most to him in the world. At supper that evening, Owen was reserved with the boy. He said only, "Have you any questions about why I sold your mare today?" Millard, shocked and saddened by the news, whispered, "No." He was then told not to go near the stables until he was given permission.

Each morning for months, Sheets remembers, he would set his alarm to awaken him early, and then he would sit at his bedroom window, watching his grandfather ride off alone. Their relationship was very circumspect during this time; almost all communication between them ceased.

Then, exactly a year later, Owen said to Millard, "Would you like to see your new horse before or after dinner?" Millard, of course, was ecstatic and, thereafter, the two renewed their close ties.

Reflecting on this experience, Sheets sees nothing exceptionally harsh about the type of discipline he received. Characteristically, he notes the pain it caused his grandfather and the benefit it did him in the development of his own self-discipline. "I believe authority of this kind is good for everyone. The world needs this. Our emotions often seem to run contrary to good sense."

In retrospect, Sheets recalls his early life with great fondness. "I had a marvelous relationship with my whole family, including my aunts' children." Lewis Owen, by virtue of the strength of his personality and the depth of reciprocated love for his grandson, exerted a great deal of influence in the forming of Millard Sheets's adult nature. In addition to the more prosaic financial and material support given the child, the Owen family gave him their undivided emotional backing. Anything positive that Millard wanted to attempt received their whole-hearted support. He was provided with a rich and fertile medium in which to develop the talent and self-confidence that have carried him so very far.

By contrast, Sheets recalls his father, with vague affection, as "a very pleasant uncle figure." His contact with John Sheets was regular, especially after John remarried, but the strong emotional bond normally existing between a child and his biological parent instead linked Millard and his grandfather. When he was fourteen, he was called on to make a particularly wrenching decision: he was asked to choose with whom he wanted to live, Lewis Owen or John Sheets. The adolescent Sheets chose his grandfather. "My father was always very kind to me, but I simply couldn't imagine not living with my grandparents." So, he remained with them, and many of the things Owen held dear were transferred to Sheets. Perhaps the most influential was his great love for horses.

Horses—rounded bodies, elongated necks, frolicsome or wild—are familiar subjects in Sheets's work. They appear in his paintings, in his murals, and in his tapestries. Once he became financially able to acquire and house them, horses were always included in the Sheets menagerie. He designed an efficient and attractive stable and training ring for their Padua Hills property, and, until recently, horses were stabled on the grounds of Barking Rocks. Until 1980, Sheets rode regularly and is still actively involved in the breeding and raising of racehorses. Together with a partner and a trainer, Sheets has several stabled in southern California.

The Barking Rocks stable is now a storage facility, but the aviary and plant room still houses a beautiful assortment of doves, budgerigars, and other feathered creatures. Golden pheasants, fancy roosters, and hens parade in their outdoor enclosures, secure from the resident ginger-and-white cat. Sheets and his wife are now, as they have been most of their lives, surrounded by beautiful things, both animate and inanimate.

Sheets has a fascination with other places and people of other cultures, and, as a result, he has traveled a great deal. Mexico, Africa, India, the Orient, and the South Pacific have all provided him with material for his work. The lushness of their landscapes and the mysteries of their people have acted as magnets for Sheets's questing imagination. Many of his trips are connected with the painting workshops he has led. Before his retirement from active participation in his design studio, he also spent a great deal of time in various parts of the world working on projects.

The subjects, people, and societies of some of Sheets's best-known works are considered primitive to most Americans. Sheets, on the contrary, sees these groups as far more advanced than American civilization. Sheets's definition of civilization is the thoroughness with which individuals are able to adapt to their circumstances. In his estimation, Americans, while technologically superior to most of the world, remain far behind the Mexicans, the Tahitians, and the Africans in their ability to cope with their physical and cultural environment.

In painting these people and their landscapes, Sheets uses colors whose intensity resonates. While the backgrounds are sometimes neutral tones, brilliant shades highlight these compositions, punctuating the works with an arresting effect. He uses clear colors, pushed to incredible strength; his creative state-

IN THE HILL COUNTRY
OF MOOREA
watercolor 30 x 40 inches 1982

ments are also clear and uncomplicated.

Standing in startling contrast to this general approach are the paintings Sheets did during and after World War II. A war correspondent for *Life* magazine, Sheets chose to go to the China-Burma-India (C-B-I) theater. His experiences there were both horrifying and enlightening, and the art that resulted is accentuated with somber, deep-toned meditations in oil and watercolor. Witnessing both the destruction of life and starvation on a large scale, Sheets's perspective of the world widened and his work of that period reflected a new level of maturity and emotion. "During the fighting and the time I spent in the C-B-I theater, I was too shaken and intellectually stunned to do any complete paintings," Sheets says. "I made many, many sketches, though, as well as a real effort to remember each scene that particularly affected me. Then, once I returned to America, I painted frantically, for months, exorcising the demons."

Art, in all its myriad forms, is such an integral part of this man that it is difficult to separate it from either his personal or his professional life. Sheets's home is filled with it; in addition, a magnificent gallery is part of the Barking Rocks estate. The gallery houses many rare and beautiful treasures of sculpture, paintings, drawings, tapestries, and icons, all beautifully dis-

THE MOURNER
charcoal   17 x 21 inches   1943

played for the maximum benefit and enjoyment of the viewer. Gathered during Sheets's travels over the years, his collection reflects the scope of his interests and the fundamental significance he places upon art. He says he cannot remember a time when he did not want to be a painter and when he was not interested in the aesthetics of his surroundings. This intensity of delight in creativity has not lessened with age and experience. If anything, it seems to have expanded, reaching new levels as Sheets's grasp of art and its possibilities enlarged.

Millard Sheets's interest in drawing was stimulated very early in life, when his aunts entertained him by first drawing pictures for him and then giving him materials and showing him how he, too, could make pictures. Every effort he made was praised and rewarded. As early as seven, he had his first painting lesson, from a neighbor, whom he paid with his own quarters. She saw him one day, peering in at her through an open door while she painted. Although strictly an amateur and a copyist, she was happy to share her knowledge with the small boy, teaching him to use a palette knife and a brush and to mix colors.

In 1919, Sheets entered his first competition, the copy division of the Los Angeles County Fair fine arts show. The fair, held annually in Pomona and initiated by his uncle Louis Sheets, gave Millard an opportunity to show his work—in this case, a copy of a tinted photograph of Lake Kilarney. When he learned that he had won first prize in his division, he raced to the exhibit to experience the thrill of seeing his work hung with its blue ribbon.

It was at this time that he had an initially startling but eventually fortuitous meeting with an established professional artist, Theodore B. Modra, one of the most important figures in Sheets's early art apprenticeship. Modra tapped Sheets on the shoulder and demanded sternly, "Are you the person who painted this picture?" When Millard admitted that he was indeed the culprit, Modra led the frightened boy into his office, where he lectured him on the sins of copying.

Modra's appearance was almost a caricature of what an artist should look like: short, white goatee, thick white hair, and flowing tie. His appearance notwithstanding, Modra had a keen mind, and an absolute horror of imitation. The Polish painter, director of the fair's art show, pointed out to Sheets that copying destroyed an artist's ability to think. He then offered to help the young man upgrade his talents; he asked Sheets to bring some original work to his studio for criticism.

A contemporary of artists such as George Bellows, George Luks, and John Sloan, Modra had come to Pomona from New York to retire and raise oranges. He was pulled back into the art world when Louis Sheets, co-founder and president of the first Los Angeles County Fair, asked Modra to direct the art portion of the fair.

A door had been opened for Sheets, and he was invited to investigate horizons he had not known existed. Modra did not teach Sheets particular techniques; rather, he stimulated the young boy to think about art. Himself a student of Robert Henri, Modra gave the young man one Saturday a month for three years. During this time, the painter and his wife would take Sheets to Laguna Beach, where Modra and Sheets would sleep on the sand, talk, and work, painting from nature. Sheets says it was one of those experiences that could only happen with the good fortune of meeting the right person at the right time.

Helen Daggs, a junior high school art teacher, also had an important influence on Sheets during these years. A graduate of Pomona College, Daggs taught Sheets to approach art with an eye toward the underlying form of objects. "She wasn't a great artist herself," Sheets remembers, "but she had a wonderful ability to show us a fundamental approach to structure—an approach that stayed with me." Daggs took her classes for walks in the nearby hills and encouraged them to draw and observe nature, concentrating on the details of form to establish a firm understanding of the object. Sheets still treasures the memory of Helen Daggs and the depth of her feeling for art.

Sheets's burgeoning talent was recognized while he was in high school by yet another teacher, Ida Webster. A Latin instructor, Webster moved to art when Latin was dropped from the curriculum. She persuaded the principal to give Sheets released time from his studies to paint. Because he had done well in his classes and was ahead of schedule in credits, Sheets was given the afternoons to practice and explore his talent.

When Millard Sheets was sixteen, he entered one of his paintings in the Laguna Beach Art Association competition. Attracted by the climate and scenery, many established artists migrated to this area, and the Laguna Beach Art Association was one of the first of its kind to be established in California. Its membership was a solid one. Once a year, a show was held to which nonmembers were invited to submit their work to a jury. After Sheets's painting was accepted, he was viewing the exhibit and experienced a sense of *déjà vu* when once again a gentleman inquired whether or not he was Millard Sheets. When the boy responded, the very tall, distinguished man introduced himself: Clarence Hinkle, an artist with a fine reputation in both Paris and New York art circles.

Thus a second pivotal relationship began, one that would have far-reaching effects on Sheets's approach to his work. Sheets made the three-hour trip from Pomona to Laguna once a month, and Hinkle taught Sheets about design and color. He introduced the young artist to a new concept: the importance of the underlying abstract structure which must be present in every painting, regardless of style. Under Hinkle's direction, Sheets honed his native skills for making quick decisions about composition and organization of material. He often painted outside, using very large canvasses. The practicality of this would have been undermined if Sheets had not been able to come to grips with the picture immediately. Hinkle taught him to cope with such problems, to set the color chord and value range quickly.

The painting entered in the Laguna Beach show was purchased by an author whom Sheets had idolized since he had discovered his books several years before. Will Levington Comfort wrote of the Orient and India, where he had lived. Sheets was reading his book, *Mid-Stream,* at the time. After purchasing Sheets's work, he called the sixteen-year-old artist to tell him how much he liked it. As a result, Sheets was eventually able to meet Comfort in person. Their friendship grew and continued until the author's death. That he had met Hinkle and had spoken to Will Comfort, both in the same day, were invaluable experiences to Sheets. As a result of his first professional art show acceptance, Sheets developed emotional ties with far-reaching consequences. Art had brought him to people with ideas and creativity, and Sheets valued that most of all.

People are extremely important to Millard Sheets. While not everyone responds to his personality, many are enchanted by him. He acquires friends and makes every effort to keep them.

Privately, Millard Sheets is very much a family man. He and his wife have four children (all of whom have grown to become productive and creative adults) as well as seventeen grandchildren. Their home has always been the center of family activity. Each summer, most of the children and grandchildren spend as much time as they can with Millard and Mary at Barking Rocks. The affection between parents and offspring and between husband and wife is obvious. Mary says that her regard for her husband has grown steadily through the fifty-three years they have spent together, creating a "very special way of life."

Sheets has experienced all the joys, the challenges, the tensions, and the occasional conflicts of a healthy, vigorous family life. With six strong-minded and creative individualists living and growing up together, there were bound to be disagreements and decided differences of opinion; yet, it was a household abounding in warmth and fun and laughter.

Millard Owen Sheets, Jr., the oldest son, known as Owen to avoid confusion, is an agronomist for a large Hawaiian sugar-cane plantation, Hamakua Mill Company. He gives his father full credit for making the connection that started him in this career. While on a ship bound for Hawaii, Sheets spoke with a fellow traveler who told him about an excellent program available through the University of Hawaii; Owen was the beneficiary of this information, electing to attend the school and pursue his work in plantation management through the graduate level. Personally, Owen feels that he has "a pretty good combination" of his parents' qualities: his father's spirit of adventure, and his mother's caution.

Carolyn Owen-Towle, the Sheetses' second child, claims that both of her parents have greatly influenced her life. Her father's exuberant, demonstrative affection, balanced by his clear-cut ethical principles, was transmitted to all of his children. Carolyn is a Unitarian Universalist minister, and, therefore, she has ample opportunity to make use of these qualities. Her father's philosophy that "we are here for a purpose, which is to give our all back to life, for what we have been so richly given," is deeply ingrained.

David Baskerville Stary-Sheets is a tall, quietly strong person with a complete lack of guile. He has approached his life with a positive attitude, his father's legacy. A furniture designer, David has internalized his father's dictum that attitude will have more impact on a project's outcome than any other one factor. He also notes his father's expectation that each of his children surpasses his own highest achievements. Sheets's example has enabled his third child to tap wells of inner strength.

John Anthony Sheets is a sculptor and architectural designer in Pasadena, California. Although he says he spent the first thirty years of his life trying to be different than his father, Tony was spurred to work in creative mediums after his father prodded him to become serious about his talents. Sheets, says Tony, has tremendous insight in all areas of art and design;

that insight, coupled with his father's capacity for teaching, enabled Tony to make use of his greatest creative efforts.

A third generation of artists in the family is beginning, as Owen's son, Timothy, studies with his grandfather at Barking Rocks. Sheets tries to restrain his delight, but it is easily noticeable. He was the young man's teacher-of-choice, and Sheets says he is a quick learner with a natural gift and feeling for art. It is clear that the sessions the two share are very important to Sheets.

Mary Baskerville Sheets, the wife and mother of this sometimes tempestuous group, left her study of art in 1929, during her last semester at UCLA, to marry Sheets. She recalls that her family was initially opposed to her decision, but came to value Millard a great deal. She has no regrets about her choice; her husband and her children seem to be the delight of her life, and she is fiercely protective and supportive. "My way of life with Millard has been a true adventure: challenging, exhilarating, fulfilling, hectic, blessed, always with a never-failing love. While we share fundamental values and beliefs in the meaning and purpose of our lives, we are decidedly different in personality. He is the ultimate optimist, bold and dauntless, and impatient with mundane details; I am cautious, a worrier who needs order and solvency." Mary cites Sheets's strength, determination, resilience, and his philosophy of affirmation. "He has suffered all his life with cruel headaches; he's had his share of serious illnesses and disappointments, yet he does not brood. If a project he has worked on does not materialize, he believes it is not meant to be, and goes on to the next challenge." Of their enduring marriage, Mary is equally affirmative. "The greatest joy of all

has been his love for the children, his friendship with them, and his pride in their accomplishments. As for me, he enfolds me still in a love as tender and protective as he did in those blissful days over a half-century ago."

Mary was introduced to Sheets by her sister, Elizabeth Baskerville McNaughton. Beth was a student at Chouinard's and was part of the Sheets-Dike group. She was pleased when her younger sister and Sheets married, and has remained the couple's closest friend. She characterizes Sheets as a whirlwind. "Don't try to keep up, just relax and enjoy his tremendous zest for living, his creativity, his own feeling of awe in the presence of beauty, and his spiritual response. There's no one like him, and there's not likely to be soon."

Filtered through these various subjective perspectives, Millard Sheets emerges with several distinct and constant features. The overwhelming one is love. It infuses him and his work and is a significant part of his personal and professional life. It is his love for beauty and humanity that serves as the source of his optimism, zest, and creativity. In the end, his strong will and forceful character—sometimes a source of difficulty when his children were adolescents—has enabled him to carry his love to the world. Through his art, designs, and teaching, he has enriched the environment and enlarged the perspectives of everyone with whom he has come in contact—no matter how superficially.

One of his designs is Barking Rocks, an outgrowth of Sheets's vision. Millard and Mary first saw the area in 1959, while en route from a friend's house, where Millard had gone to paint the redwood forest they owned. Sheets immediately decided that he must have some of the property along the majestic sweep of coastline on which they stood. After a great deal of discussion, and a very adventurous airplane ride, Sheets located the only real estate broker in Anchor Bay, California, who was in turn able to sell him the only property for sale along the entire Mendocino coastline. In 1960, Barking Rocks was created, a monument to a man's drive and determination and a retreat from the demands placed upon him by his many careers.

These careers began with one step—from high school to art school. Art school had not been considered by Sheets's father, John. He had offered to pay Millard's college tuition, but withdrew the offer when his son, upon reevaluating his ambitions, decided upon Chouinard's School of Art instead. This reevaluation came in the light of Modra and Hinkle's advice that Sheets should obtain the best formal art training possible. Universities, at that time, had neither the teachers nor the equipment to provide such training, nor did they possess the vision to provide the facilities.

John Sheets could never seem to understand his son's fascination with art, which he considered an incredibly risky field. Conservative by nature, he was fearful of venturing beyond the point of "playing it safe" with a salaried job. While Sheets maintains that he and his father were close, it seems as though there was a wide gulf of understanding between them, natural in the circumstances. Sheets was a visitor in his father and stepmother's home, not a member of it. He took his primary guidance from his grandparents. John Sheets was undoubtedly not aware of the central

importance art played in his son's life, and, not wanting to encourage an impractical endeavor, chose not to pay for Millard's art education. So it was Sheets's uncle, Chauncy Perrin, who provided for his first semester at Chouinard's.

Now philosophical about his father's attitude, Sheets says that long before he died, his father learned to be happy about his son's involvement in art. He values his father, but feels fortunate in being raised by his grandparents, who never wavered in their support of him.

Millard Sheets's life can be accurately summed up in the words of Geoffry Keynes, who, in his book *The Gates of Memory,* described his own life as "a quite outrageously enjoyable existence." Sheets's irrepressible spirit has kept him going even when it would have been understandable for him to stop or, at least, slow down. Stricken by a serious illness in 1980, one that required several weeks of treatment, he still managed to lecture, serve on art juries, attend gallery openings on the East Coast, and lead innumerable workshops—one of them, a Hewitt affair, took him and his wife, Mary, far outside the United States to Hong Kong and China.

During this period, Sheets and Mary were also involved with the production of *A West African Journal,* the account of their 1979 trip to Senegal, Mali, Upper Volta, and the Ivory Coast. Mary authored the book and Millard illustrated it with evocative black-and-white line drawings. The story recounts their experiences and reflections of what they saw as well as the exotic environment through which they were traveling. The couple's enthusiasm radiates throughout the volume.

It is difficult to convey in a brief statement the extent of Sheets's spirit; it pervades every aspect of his life and work and yet it is fleeting and difficult to grasp.

His activities in the face of—perhaps in spite of—a physically and mentally painful situation exemplify his very real affirmation of life. This affirmation is painted into his art, woven into his tapestries, and mortared into each of the buildings he has designed.

MILLARD SHEETS

· VARIATIONS · ON · A · THEME ·

CAMEROON MARKET, AFRICA *watercolor 30 x 40 inches 1982*

VARIATIONS ON A THEME: ARTIST

PAINTINGS BY MILLARD SHEETS SEEM TO GLOW. The source of that light is not always discernible: is it the colors that he uses, or the spirit with which he executes each piece? Sheets has never been preoccupied with reproducing exact replications of scenes; instead, he has sought to capture the rhythmic configurations that underlie the landscape and its inhabitants.

His paintings also display an emotional power, whether they depict a sunny California landscape, a whirling African marketplace, or a scene of dark emotion, such as the 1982 painting entitled *Night of the Dead*. A product of one of Sheets's many trips to Mexico, this watercolor—startling for the intensity and clarity of tone—demonstrates Sheets's ability to go beyond superficial representationalism to the heart of an ancient and devout ceremony. Women are the primary participants in this annual observance; they prepare food and drink for the spirits of departed loved ones, and sit in communal, night-long vigil upon the cold ground. Dough molded into the shape

of skulls is the most traditional staple, and wine or beer in shallow bowls completes the ceremonial repast. Candles flicker eerily in the darkness, marking vigil sites where women silently wait, maintained by the depth of their faith. *Night of the Dead* is characteristic of Sheets's capability to see beyond the surface and capture the emotion as well as the form of a subject.

Gloria-Gilda Deák succinctly dissects Sheets's approach in a 1982 Kennedy Galleries catalog of his work:

Paintings by Sheets are characterized by a vivid surface rhythm in which loosely drawn shapes are harmoniously contained within wide areas of color and texture. There is a distinct tilt in the direction of realistic projection, but there is a stronger tilt in the direction of what Sheets defines as the perceptive powers of the artist. If the essence of a subject calls for geometric principles, then forms will be pushed toward abstractions, and human figures may wear an androgynous air. Sketchiness becomes an evocative pictorial device. When forms are placed close to the forefront of the picture plane, and space is defined through a series of tonal vibrations, an effect is created of a vivid tapestry. More often than not, the compositional elements in a Sheets painting are strong and well defined, and colors applied in a wide spectrum of deep tones. But whether the subject is realistically rendered or offered in terms of an emphasis on forms, one responds to the lively designs inherent in the rendering, and to the clear powerful colors that are the hallmark of his work.*

The evolution of this style has taken place over the last sixty years. Sheets has always had the skill to create, but, as he observes, "Skill is a means, not an end." Painting is for him an articulation of the earth, a search for the underlying values that illuminate life. Ultimately, it is a means to express those emotions which cannot be communicated in any other medium. Sheets has an intense love for the world and its curiosities, and his work reflects this. He abhors the superficial approach in all things, especially art; as a result, the skill to recreate what the eye sees is insignificant to him. "The eye cannot think, cannot feel the underlying quality of the life that surrounds us. The mind must do that, and that is where the abstract painters excel. Impressionists paved the way for them to or-

_____
*From *The Paintings of Millard Sheets* © 1982 by Kennedy Galleries, Inc., New York.

ganize every shape, color, and line. Modern abstract art is a victory of the mind over the eye." Sheets admires many of the abstractionist painters, and, as a young man, was excited by the impressionists, particularly Monet, van Gogh, and Gauguin. His own work can be characterized as representational, heavily imbued with sound abstractionist undertones.

The search for depth and intent through his art is important to Sheets. After some twenty years of painting, he experienced a philosophical crisis. Why, he wondered, could he not advance beyond a particular point in his work? Glibness comes easily to those who have mastered technique, and Sheets felt that he was in danger of relying too much upon his well-established skills. "It is important to go beyond what you know you can do, to continue to learn and experiment. In the last ten years I feel I've made great strides in my work because I've challenged myself." Sheets invents artistic challenges for himself, and then meets and overcomes them. The most universal solution he has found is love. That, and his tremendous excitement about the world, continually drives him to plumb the depths of his creativity.

Skill, mastery of technique, and love: these are the elements of a potent combination that Sheets has developed over the span of his career. His work can be found in more than forty public and private collections, a reflection on the success Sheets has had in utilizing his inborn and developed talent. He has also had an important impact on others, leading the way to a fresh approach and reconsideration of the watercolor medium.

Sheets's formal art instruction began in September 1925 at Chouinard's School of Art in Los Angeles, California. Eager to begin study, he and a friend, Harold Graham, took the bus into the city and stopped first at the Los Angeles Art Institute. "Something about the school didn't feel right," Sheets says. "There were lots of students and the work they were doing was certainly interesting, but I didn't feel that the institute would be the right place for me." Their next visit was to Chouinard's, where the atmosphere was much more attractive to the young men. "Chouinard's seemed exactly right from the moment we were welcomed at the door."

Nelbert Chouinard was the moving power behind this precarious but energetic educational venture. Her school was housed in a ramshackle, two-story frame building that had been haphazardly refurbished. A lopsided barnlike structure was in back of the main building, whose lackluster façade belied the friendliness and inspiration that was contained within its walls.

The staff included Patti Patterson, teacher of design; draftsman and instructor Lawrence Murphy; and the erudite F. Tolles Chamberlain. It was Chamberlain who was to become a strong influence in Sheets's career.

Chamberlain had traveled widely in Europe as a two-time Prix de Rome student winner; he had a truly phenomenal knowledge of art. A distinguished man, he would glance at students over his pince-nez with their dangling black silk ribbon, and his words would tumble over one another in his excitement and eagerness to share his knowledge with his students. Chamberlain was particularly informed on mural painting, on the Renaissance and later European painters, and on Chinese art.

In Sheets, Chamberlain discovered a kindred spirit, not as informed, but certainly as eager to learn. Sheets had a special fascination with mural painting, and no one knew more about it than Chamberlain. He spoke of it with rapture. As a result of the enthusiasm displayed by several of the students, Sheets among them, Chamberlain formed a special class to teach mural painting to these dedicated few. The classes met one evening a week in the barn behind the main building, after the regular sessions were over. Chamberlain showed the students incredible reproductions of murals from Europe and other parts of the world. He would assign problems, on which they would work on their own time. Most of all, he shared himself and his experience with the students. "I'm sure he wasn't paid for this," Sheets observed. "He just gave his time and we were so happy to be with him that there never seemed to be time enough."

It was at Chouinard's that Sheets met Phil Dike, a shy, thin boy. Sheets and Dike took to one another immediately, an odd combination due to the wide divergence of their natures; Sheets was friendly and outgoing with an athletic build and a sheer fascination with adventure. Yet they became fast friends, and before long were painting and sketching together.

At this time, Los Angeles was something of a cultural wasteland, with very little fine art for the students to see. Instead, they studied the work of Homer and Whistler, Bridgeman, and the English watercolor school. Sheets saw—earlier than the rest of them, Dike says—the potential of the simple California scenes. He learned how to make them more dynamic, using their unique qualities of light and form. His ideas and skills were solidifying into a distinctly individual method and style.

They worked diligently in Chamberlain's classes devoted to figure drawing, landscape, and still life. Their after-hours study of murals required a great deal of time and concentration also. Murals-in-progress were scattered throughout the old barn and filled the courtyard that was Chouinard's rear lot. Not a superficial study class, it demanded the students' full attention. Chamberlain instructed them in the technical aspects of mural design and painting, stimulating aesthetic ideas into tangible form.

Sheets's introduction to architecture came through this process. Today, he considers it among the most marvelous four or five years of his life. "Working with a great teacher and a marvelous collection of fellow students was a terrific opportunity. It was a great period for people working together."

During this same period, Sheets began working with architects, doing delineations, or renderings. He also started a night class in etching for artists and architects. From the friendships he began in these classes, many mural projects were born: two early commissions came in 1931–1932. One was to design and execute a mural for a reception room in Robinson's Department Store and the other a fresco for Bullock's Men's Store, both in Los Angeles.

The mural for Robinson's was executed in transparent oil paint on a toned hardwood wall; it created a strong tapestry-like effect upon the natural wood. The fresco for Bullock's was described by the store as a pure design, symbolizing work, opportunity, and progress in the manufacture of men's clothing of the future.

His next major commission came during 1932 when he was asked to paint frescoes for the courtyard of the Pasadena Junior High School. The results of his efforts attracted critical attention, almost for the first time. The subjects were *The Farm* and *The Harbor,* and he hired James Patrick as his assistant. Sheets

often enlisted the aid of his friends in projects, but as Phil Paradise, a fellow student, noted, Sheets usually worked for so little that many of them could not afford to make a practice of helping him.

The school's principal was Derwood Baker, a forward-looking person who was familiar with Sheets's work as a muralist. Working almost every night for a year, Sheets and Patrick did the two large figurative panels in a true Italianate fresco form: transparent oils on plaster. They covered the walls a section at a time with very dry plaster and worked on it until it oxidized. Once oxidized, the plaster would not absorb any more water or pigment. If they had not completed their work on the oxidized section, they had to scratch off the surface, replaster, and begin again. The rain was also a problem. Often Sheets and Patrick worked under canvas, their work area illuminated by light bulbs strung on wire.

Art critic Arthur Millier gave the dedication address when the work was finished. After commenting on the frescoes themselves, he predicted that "When the world pays [Sheets] his dues, you will say 'It was here he began.' "

Sheets's reputation grew and endured, but the murals he painted for the Pasadena school did not fare so well. In the interest of preserving the murals from the weather, the custodian mixed a very heavy concentration of castile soap and water and put it on the painted walls. "It looked like someone had been pouring milk over them for months. The color was destroyed," Sheets recalls. The artist did not know of the damage; the principal changed and the new man did not inform Sheets of what had happened. Eventually, another general custodian decided the thing to do was to paint them over with cement paint. Fifteen years later they called Sheets, hoping he could suggest a method of restoration. This proved to be impossible; experts dug into the cement covering and found, by picking the cement off very slowly with small scalpels, that the paint had been so damaged that there would be no value in proceeding. Sheets still regrets that he has no good photographs of these three early mural efforts.

Sheets valued Chamberlain's guidance and instruction in the craft of painting murals, as well as in other areas. However, his admiration and reverence for the man was sometimes overshadowed by his own curiosity about people and ways that were unfamiliar to him.

The gypsy cycle of canvasses was one of the most ambitious projects of the artist's early years and the result of this curiosity. In 1927 he missed Chamberlain's classes for several weeks. Instead of attending his scheduled sessions, Sheets went to the Whittier Narrows, outside of Los Angeles. Here, all the gypsies in the United States had congregated, meeting to select a new queen. Their colorful costumes, horses, brightly painted wagons and tents, and other trappings attracted Sheets like magnets. Each day he carried his canvasses and paints to the Narrows; he did large (40-by-40-inch) paintings right on the spot. The gypsies were suspicious when the young man first appeared, but they gradually came to accept his presence. The paintings were a success, but Chamberlain was very stern with Sheets when the younger man finally returned to class.

During the time Sheets was painting murals and his gypsy canvasses, he was also entering every art exhibit he heard about. Often, he encouraged others to do the same, helping them when he could. Sheets submitted work to Santa Cruz, the Pennsylvania Academy of Art, the Art Institute of Chicago—any place that held oil or watercolor shows.

He worked diligently, and his efforts were noted by Dalzell Hatfield, owner, with Bert Newhouse, of an art gallery on West Eighth Street, not far from Chouinard's. Sheets had often admired the gallery's display of the impressionist and post-impressionist painters such as van Gogh and Matisse and others not well known in 1927.

Hatfield phoned Sheets at Chouinard's one day that year and asked him to come to the gallery. Voicing his admiration for the young man's work, Hatfield offered to represent him. Hatfield said that it was very difficult for an artist to survive until he had created and sold a substantial body of work—one hundred or so paintings. Since Sheets was just beginning his career, it would be some time before he had reached that point. Hatfield felt, though, that they could both benefit by their association.

Sheets was elated; he was invigorated by the prospect of the hard work that Hatfield said would be necessary to achieve success. Their association was ultimately to last forty-six years, during which time Dalzell Hatfield and his wife, Ruth, sold over 3,600 of Sheets's paintings. "The same elements that go into making a good marriage also go into a successful artist-gallery relationship. There must be an initial respect and the artist must contribute something to the relationship," Sheets says. A man who does not take commitments lightly, the artist developed an almost inexpressible respect and affection for the Hatfields, who he felt were absolutely dedicated to their artists. Their faith, judgment, understanding, and love for Sheets as both an artist and an individual are still important to him.

HORSES AND GOLDEN HILLS
OF CALIFORNIA
acrylic   30 x 40 inches   1981

One of the ways in which Hatfield supported Sheets early in their relationship was by sponsoring his first one-man show in 1929. Sheets had almost two years to prepare, and he painted with the fervor of a man possessed: watercolors, oils, etchings, and drawings. By the time Hatfield was ready to open the show, Sheets had assembled a wide range of work for a comprehensive exhibit.

The first public showing in the Newhouse Gallery, as it was then called, was a critical and financial success. Sheets was particularly touched by Bert New-house's purchase of the first painting. The exhibit was favorably reviewed by the art critics of the *Los Angeles Times,* as well as other Los Angeles papers. Merle Armitage sounded an encouraging note in the *Los Angeles Record:* "I am beginning to get more enthusiastic about the new developments in art and younger painters in southern California. Emerging from the sea of the commonplace are a few strong artists with something to say . . . now comes Millard Sheets. This youngster of twenty-one is a born painter . . . he has a facility and verve found in men twice his age.

Here is a man who can paint California without banality and sentimentality." Armitage went on to say that Sheets seemed to him destined to be one of California's artistic emancipators.

Armitage's prediction proved to be accurate. Sheets's development into one of the premier artists of his time, as foreseen by Armitage and others, was closely followed by area art critics.

Sheets believes that critics in the early days of his career served an important purpose. Then, the critics concerned themselves with education of the public through their reviews, stimulating public awareness of art. Critics also helped to educate artists, by telling them where they were in their development. Today, except for a handful of national critics, inept judgment is the norm; an intellectual indulgence predominates, a showing off of superficial perception, Sheets says.

Good, bad, or indifferent, criticism has seldom affected Millard Sheets. He developed his talent on his own timetable, traveling ever further on his personal creative continuum.

Another milestone in this progress came in 1929 when Sheets was invited to compete in the Edward B. Davis competition at the Witte Museum in San Antonio, Texas. Large cash prizes were offered and that, in tandem with the benefits of participation in a major show, whetted Sheets's competitive appetite even more. The painting, sent by Ruth Hatfield in error, was entitled *The Goat Ranch*. It won second prize in the Davis competition, and Sheets was awarded $1,750, a princely sum in that spring before the stock market crashed.

At twenty-two, Sheets had experienced the success of his first one-man show and of winning a substantial cash prize in an important competition. This allowed him to realize his long-held dream: he would go to Europe and see the great art treasures his mentors had described to him so vividly.

Before he left for Europe, two propitious events took place; both had a significant impact on Sheets's future. He met Mary Baskerville, sister of Chouinard student Beth Baskerville, in Palm Springs, and he met architect Cass Gilbert in New York City. A continent apart, these meetings determined new directions for Millard Sheets.

Reluctant to leave California after meeting Mary Baskerville, Sheets nevertheless left Los Angeles on a banana boat with a friend, Bill Veale, on June 1, 1929. The trip, financed by the proceeds from the one-man show and the Davis prize, was a long one by today's standards, but perfect for an artist. The ship stopped at seventeen Central and South American ports, where it took at least a day to unload cargo. During each stop—Mazatlan, Mexico; La Libertad, Guatemala; Costa Rica; El Salvador; Cartagena, Colombia; Havana, Cuba—Sheets dashed off the ship and painted frantically, trying to capture the life he saw taking place around him. He also sent dozens of letters to Mary.

At last they docked in New York. Through a California architect whom he had taught in a night class on etching, Sheets was invited to see Cass Gilbert, the man who had designed some of the first New York skyscrapers, including the then-new Woolworth Building. Gilbert greeted him most cordially, gave him a tour of the offices, and took him to a sumptuous lunch at his club. During the lunch, they discussed architecture and the great opportunities awaiting Sheets in Europe. Noting the young man's rapt response,

DINAN, FRANCE *sketch* 1929

Gilbert encouraged him to draw the marvelous buildings he would see everywhere. Sheets told him that he had done very little architectural drawing, but Gilbert continued to emphasize the value of his suggestion. He impressed upon Sheets the tremendous chance the latter had to experiment in a field that overflowed with challenge. "There is no way I can ever repay the unselfish gifts made to me by men like Cass Gilbert. He took time to see a very young artist and counsel him intelligently, stirring his excitement in a wholly new experience, drawing the great buildings of Europe," Sheets says today.

Fortified by this excellent advice, Sheets and Veale steamed out of New York harbor, bound for Europe. Upon arrival, Sheets, Veale, and Patti Patterson began by traveling through Holland, exploring museums. Then Veale went to the Bauhaus in Germany and Sheets met another friend, Oliver Milburn, who had rented a car. They traveled through France, Switzerland, Italy, and Spain. Everywhere he went, Sheets drew meticulous renditions of the magnificent Gothic structures he saw all around him in the ancient cities and towns they explored.

Sheets was drawn to museums, and it was during this trip that he saw his first original Rembrandts and Vermeers. He was stunned by their intensity of emotion, clarity of color, and excellence of technique. The humanity their work displayed moved Sheets and his companions. He was also entranced by the earlier Renaissance paintings he saw; the symbolism they employed struck a deep responsive chord within him. Although he was anxious to see impressionist and post-impressionist paintings, he found that no special museum housed them, and none were to be found in the more traditional collections.

While in Paris, Sheets successfully searched for the master printer Gaston Dorfinant, in order to learn about lithography, as no one on the West Coast was involved in this medium then. When he located Dorfinant's studio, up several flights of stairs in a fourteenth-century building, he was welcomed into a chaotic room full of people. In a nearby studio, Henri Matisse worked. Dorfinant's equipment and skill produced striking results, and Sheets observed the various processes included in creating a lithograph. As he began to grasp the rudiments, he experimented himself, drawing on a stone plate. To his surprise, Dorfinant poured gum arabic on the plate and then washed it off, image and all. Indignation turned to delight when, with a few passes of an ink roller, his drawing reappeared. Dorfinant and the other students were amused by Sheets's reaction, and toasted him with red wine and laughter.

Within days of arriving at the printing studio, Sheets took the opportunity presented him and entered a painting in the competition of the *Societe du Salon d'Automne* (Autumn Salon). Undaunted by an almost impossible deadline of three days, Sheets submitted *Women of Champerico*. He was motivated by the advice offered him before coming to Europe: get into a Paris salon show. With characteristic confidence, he did so at the first opportunity. It ultimately took the group five months to decide on the paintings they would include in their fall exhibition—*Women of Champerico* was one of them. Notified of his acceptance, Sheets called the United States immediately to share the news with his family.

Not long afterward, Sheets left Europe for America and Mary.

He had a stormy ocean crossing, and was glad to see the New York harbor come into view. His first stop after disembarking was at Cass Gilbert's office, where he showed the architect the work he had done. Gilbert was delighted with the results of his suggestion to Sheets and promptly called the editors of two prominent professional magazines, *Architectural Record* and *Pencil Points*. At Gilbert's insistence, and because they were equally impressed with the young artist's work, these men ran feature stories on Sheets and his work. "These were threads upon which my future life was woven. That introduction to the professional journals of American architects was of unlimited importance throughout the rest of my career. As a result, I was able to move freely around the country and make contacts. To this day, new friends remind me of them."

Sheets took a train from New York to Los Angeles, arriving in California on December 16; Mary Baskerville met him at the station. He had long ago realized the intensity of his feeling for her, and they had an emotional reunion. In a whirlwind of decision-making, they finalized their wedding plans and on April 25, 1930, they were married.

Although they had little in a material sense, much of his grandfather's spirit of derring-do seemed to have rubbed off on Sheets, and he and Mary began their married life with soaring spirits. He set high goals for himself and then moved as rapidly as possible toward them, managing to remain one jump ahead of his obligations. They loved beautiful things—plants, animals, birds, art—everything that added to life's sentiment and visual pleasures, and he started to collect them.

In his pursuit of the funds with which to accommodate this passion, he occasionally came to grief.

Mary Baskerville and Millard Sheets, 1930; they began their married life with soaring spirits.

Sheets accepted a commission from a group that wanted a mural for their new institution, the Hollywood Savings and Loan Company. Sheets hired assistants, rented a studio, and prepared preliminary drawings after receiving a third of the commission in advance. The murals were completed but Sheets had not received the balance when Beesemyer, the main officer of the company, was arrested for manipulation of depositors' funds. This meant financial ruin for hundreds of families and left Sheets with the obligation to pay the salaries of the men he had hired and the rent for the loft studio. In addition, his own savings had been in a branch of the Hollywood Savings and Loan Company. It was a dark time for the young couple, but one to which Sheets responded in a characteristic manner. Over a period of time, he paid off all of his debts and threw himself into other projects, ones with more stability.

The years following his return from Europe and his marriage to Mary were vital to Sheets's growth and development as an artist. Despite the Depression, 1930 to 1939 was a period of substantial gain for him and for many California artists.

The California watercolor school, a loose association of young West Coast artists that included Dike and Sheets, began to attract national attention because of the way its adherents utilized the medium. For the most part, watercolor had formerly implied a light pencil drawing filled in or brushed over with transparent washes of color. These California artists, however, were using watercolor full strength, flowing wash over brilliant wash. Their landscapes, seascapes, and cityscapes sparkled with the brightness of a California day in full sunlight. They were an innovative group, and Sheets was their unsolicited bellwether.

Bold paintings of his native Pomona Valley, as well as other subjects, were frequently compared to the work of Winslow Homer, and they took viewers by surprise.

In 1937, after six years of participating in exhibits there, the Art Institute of Chicago invited Sheets to fill a small gallery with his paintings. One of the city's art critics commented, "[His] present paintings are superb, gorgeous in color and drawing; they exude a nervous strength that is irresistible."

This strength was first noticed by New York art critic Emily Genauer of the *New York World-Telegram.* At the time of his first one-man show in New York's Milch Gallery in 1934, she had this to say: "Though Millard Sheets is making his first appearance in New York . . . his star has been in the ascendant for some time and its radiance has fallen even on the East. He is a superb draftsman, a subtle yet daring and opulent colorist, and a romantic . . . weaving intricate patterns with rhythmic, arresting, and vital figures."

In the July 15, 1935, *New York Times* review of his second East Coast show, Edward Alden Jewell acknowledged Sheets's ability: "He develops and changes with each new problem. The prizes he has won have not turned his head and he says frankly he is only acquiring a vocabulary."

The Hatfields arranged a traveling show of Sheets's work which was exhibited in thirty-four museums throughout the middle western states and down into New Orleans. A number of paintings were sold to small museums, and others were purchased by collectors directly from the exhibit.

It was also during this time that his work was exhibited at the Los Angeles County Museum of Art, the San Diego Museum, and galleries in Santa Barbara and San Francisco. Hatfield had mounted Sheets's second one-man show in 1930 and it was a commercial success, although Sheets did not think it was as good as his first in terms of quality. "They were off-the-cuff things I had done in Europe, but the public liked them."

A watershed year in many ways, 1930 saw Sheets take on one of his biggest gambles to date: he submitted a painting to the most demanding art jury in the United States, the Carnegie International Watercolor Exhibition in Pittsburgh, Pennsylvania. A world-renowned competition, the Carnegie International had never accepted the work of an artist west of the Rocky Mountains. "I wouldn't take a long shot like that on a horse," Sheets has since declared. Yet he was willing to put himself and his work on the line. The chance of acceptance was remote, particularly since this was the only juried show Carnegie mounted, and the costs were high. Nonetheless, Sheets had *Women of Cartagena* framed, built a box for it himself, and shipped it to Pennsylvania. The jury, in a unanimous decision, accepted it for inclusion in their exhibit. A signal of honor for Sheets, it also represented a real break-through for other western artists. Sheets's admission to this inner sanctum of art led the way to a more serious consideration and evaluation of the work of his West Coast contemporaries.

Women of Cartagena is a highly stylized composition of a Colombian native in a marketplace, drawn from the sketches Sheets made during his banana boat trip from Los Angeles to New York. The dark figures of the women, some in long white dresses, the form of a large black bull in the background, together with other dark accents weave a pattern that moves in the painting's plane like an exotic dance rhythm.

Once accepted by the eastern art establishment, Sheets's work received further critical attention and, until its termination, he was invited each year to participate in the Carnegie International.

Sheets made many trips to New York during the thirties; he went there to consult with the Milch Gallery (a gallery with which the Hatfields had connected him) and to paint. While in the city, he also had stimulating discussions with other prominent artists; he affectionately remembers this period of his life. "I can't stress strongly enough how helpful the New York artists of that time were to me. Eugene Speicher, Edward Bruce, Charles Burchfield, Leon Kroll—they all took me under the wing of their knowledge and experience."

The combination of the economic conditions of the 1930s, his experiences in the East, and maturity resulted in a gradual change in Sheets's style. His usually cheerful, sunny canvasses were being replaced by somber-toned, more thoughtful paintings. Two of the most significant from this period are *Tenement Flats* and *Angel's Flight*. The first depicts a complex of tenement structures, laced into strong design by a network of rickety staircases and balconies. The buildings dwarf the human forms of the tenants. Sheets gave this painting to the Public Works of Art project, and Eleanor Roosevelt, who greatly admired it, selected *Tenement Flats* to hang in the reception hall of the White House. Later donated to the White House collection, today it is housed by the Smithsonian Institution's National Museum of American Art.

The second work, *Angel's Flight,* is important for two reasons: it exhibits a daring perspective, an off-beat study in vertigo, and its subject matter is rare for Sheets—a figure study of two young women gazing

WOMEN OF CARTAGENA   *oil   40 x 50 inches   1930*

Los Angeles County Museum of Art

ANGEL'S FLIGHT
oil   50¼ x 40 inches   1931

from their lofty perch into the dreary neighborhood below. *Angel's Flight* is now in the Los Angeles County Museum of Art.

Southern California felt the impact of Roosevelt's Public Works of Art program when, in 1934, Merle Armitage, Dalzell Hatfield, McDonald Wright, Arthur Millier and Millard Sheets, among others, were appointed to a committee to organize, select, and direct the new program in that area. Historically important throughout the United States, the Public Works of Art offered opportunities for artists to contribute and create during the depths of the Depression. Some of the nation's finest talents were given an audience and a chance to develop during this time. The committee selected ninety-five artists within a very few days and assigned them to create paintings, sculpture, murals, and graphics for the federal government, which would use them in public buildings.

Sheets continued to paint during this time, and his clear, distinct line—no fuzzy edges, no murkiness, as one critic noted—became more and more widely recognized. He exploded out of the regional-painter category and into a much larger field. While his technique and approach could be called Californian, his subject matter was cosmopolitan. Traveling occupied much of his time, too, in connection with his teaching and design responsibilities; the subjects of his works during this period reflect Sheets's experience and wide range of travels—the harbor of lower Manhattan, the deserts of the Southwest, the oil fields of Texas, and the exotic landscapes of Hawaii.

In his paintings of such tropical islands as Hawaii, the figures, boldly executed and richly colored, must compete with lush flowers and foliage. One critic described Sheets's figures this way: "Human shapes without viscera, without warmth. Yet, strangely, they have vitality." Perhaps they borrowed from Sheets's own vitality, which was comparable to a torrent, a river overflowing its banks. Beginning his days at six in the morning, Sheets did not end them until one or two the following morning. His energy cannot be disregarded when considering his enormous output of finished work.

Sheets also started painting his enormous watercolors, his "huge acquarelles," during this period of travel. They were 22 by 30 inches, a full sheet size; it was customary to use a half-sheet for watercolors. His New York dealer, Milch, wanted him to change his course and stop making these giant pictures. Sheets's gleeful reply was said to be "Nuts!"

After the rigors of the Depression and establishing a reputation in New York came Sheets's most profound experience: World War II.

The "theater of war" is a phrase that has strong emotional significance to those who have been onstage during the performance. The man who steps on this stage is never the same after the curtain falls. Whoever lives through a war matures rapidly, the process of survival is accelerated. A world-awareness is thrust upon him and his life will ever after be divided into three parts: before, during, and after the war.

Sheets's life at the time of Pearl Harbor had been one of "honey and orange blossoms," full of activity and stresses but generally peaceful. He was happily married, had four healthy children, was teaching and lecturing, both in Claremont at Scripps College and across the country, and designing murals for a wide variety of clients. He became involved in the prewar effort through his work designing air schools for the government, and was an enthusiastic advocate of a strong Allied response to Hitler's aggression. Sheets longed to participate, to aid the American war effort, and in 1943, was given that long-awaited opportunity.

The government, with the help of Philadelphian George Biddle, was assembling a cadre of artist-correspondents to cover the various theaters of the war. Biddle contacted Sheets and inquired as to his interest in participating. When Sheets assured him that he would be pleased to do his share, Biddle submitted his name to the War Department and Sheets was summoned to Washington. There, the approximately twenty artists who had been selected were briefed on the project. They were told they could choose the area to which they preferred to be sent and that they would be assigned the rank of lieutenant colonel with its attendant privileges. Not merely illustrators, they would paint as artists with an artist's interpretation of the tragedy and phenomenon of war. The War Department displayed a great deal of support for this idea and the men were duly indoctrinated and uniformed.

Sheets spent part of a sweltering New York summer waiting to be shipped abroad. One morning he opened the paper and read a very glamorized, sanitized article by Biddle on the war in Italy. This was to doom the program; two days later, Congress killed the whole project. The program was stopped in its tracks.

Recalled to Washington, D.C., Sheets was told to stay on the East Coast because the government was making arrangements with *Life* magazine to take over the project, just as it had been envisioned by the War Department. Within hours of his return to New York, Sheets received a call from Dan Longwell, the editor of *Life,* a man with great imagination, lots of fire, and a flair for accomplishment.

When Sheets and the other participants met with Longwell, they were again asked their preference for assignments. Sheets's choice of the China-Burma-India theater surprised everyone, but it reflected his ongoing fascination with the area, a fascination sparked in his childhood by Will Levington Comfort's book, *Mid-Stream.*

The next journey was back to California and his family where he waited for the Liberty ship to which he had been assigned. Liberty ships were a phenomenon of World War II; built along the Pacific coast, they were put together in twenty-nine days, loaded in fourteen, and put to sea.

The *Billy Sunday* was to be Sheets's transportation to India: by mid-July, 1943, she was ready to go. After a shakedown cruise that consisted of three round trips beyond the San Pedro Harbor to Newport and back to Los Angeles in order to determine how inaccurate the ship's compass was, the ship headed past the west end of Catalina Island and toward the South Pacific and India.

The trip was long and hazardous. At first, there were great spans of time with no pressing duties. Sheets took his turn standing watch and was immensely impressed by the panorama of the Pacific. "The nights were beautiful. Some of the fish were phosphorescent, and I could see them glide by underwater."

As the ship got closer to the South Pacific, however, the situation became much more tense. The Japanese were regularly sinking the Liberty ships, and the *Billy Sunday* was all alone, wending its way through a zig-zag course between hundreds of small islands.

There was tension on board, too, as men succumbed to fear and anxiety. Through it all, Sheets worked sketching, building furniture, and painting a mural in the crew's gallery with some of the oil paints he had brought on board with him. He transformed the wall into a scene filled with seductive mermaids coming out of the sea.

Eventually, after a series of dramatic and nerve-wracking experiences, the *Billy Sunday* landed in Hobart, Tasmania. It took a full day to go from the entrance of the harbor, up the mouth of the Dereuent River and to Hobart. There they disembarked and made the rounds of the bars. After three days of loading supplies, the ship left again. They passed through the great Australian Bight in the middle of tremendous storms. The Japanese, with their huge cruisers, regularly swept the area between Australia and Ceylon, knocking off Liberty ships with great precision. They may have been assisted by the center spread of *Reader's Digest,* which detailed the course of these American ships.

In Ceylon, the ship, with its cargo of high-octane gasoline, aerial bombs, small arms, and ammunition, headed for Madras, India. Sheets was finally approaching the land of which Will Comfort had written so enchantingly, and in Madras his expectations were fulfilled. He saw a venerable gentleman perched on top of a tall stump, ten feet off the ground. Clothed in light cotton and with a white beard that touched his stomach, the man sat there, contemplating the world. The city was filled with monks, priests, and temples. There were more people per square foot than Sheets had ever seen in his life.

Finally, they began the last leg of their trip, to Calcutta. Caught by vicious tides, the ship, still loaded with explosives, ran aground just short of a rocky cliff. It was probably their salvation to be caught in the soft sand. Sheets stood at the rail wondering what would happen next, when the captain said: "You've been wanting to go to India. Well, step off—there she is, Mother India." The ship gradually floated clear after almost a day's wait for tides and the sand-clogged condensers to clear. The balance of the trip to the mouth of the Jumna River was very slow; upon arrival, the *Billy Sunday* waited her turn to enter the river's opening and proceed to Calcutta. It had been sixty days since the ship left Los Angeles.

It took a full day of river travel to reach their goal, and what Sheets saw along the way shocked him to his very core. The ship steamed up the Jumna between lush tropical banks. Birds swooped overhead and the air was alive with insect sounds. After about twenty miles, Sheets began to notice objects floating in the water. They were bodies: "It was the most amazing combination . . . a tropical jungle background, temples, and still bodies, floating in the river. Everytime I looked around, there was another one. I'll never forget it."

India was in the grips of one of the greatest famines it had ever experienced. Thousands of people migrated to Calcutta from outlying villages, hoping to find food; as a result, the already beleaguered city was awash with the dead and the dying. Bodies were in the streets, in the gutters, and alleys.

After a terrible drought and two successive years of hurricanes, seed and almost everything else was gone. The British blamed the Bengal government, and the latter, in turn, vilified the British. The distribution of existing food supplies was deadlocked in the controversy.

FAMINE   *ink   14 x 23 inches   1944*

The first two weeks Sheets was in India, he covered the famine. Accompanied by an American officer with a jeep, he went into villages where "not a soul was alive," and jackals disposed of the dead. He was emotionally shattered by this experience; his pen sketches were later translated into paintings and drawings, which he sent back to *Life*. They were printed in the November 22, 1943, issue devoted to the famine.

After this assignment was completed, Sheets was flown to Delhi by the British. Upon his arrival, he went straight to bed, violently ill with an intestinal disorder that manifested itself with fever and dysentery. He slept for several hours and was awakened, to his surprise, by an old friend, Hal Service; he insisted that Sheets come and play a game of tennis with the viceroy of India, Lord Victor A. J. H. Lithingow, and his aide, second cousin to the king of England.

After the game, which Sheets was only able to observe, the aide took him to his wing of the viceroy's palace and into the library. There he pulled out the 1938 edition of *Millard Sheets* written by Merle Armitage and produced by a London studio. The aide, a colonel in the British army, turned out to be an avid watercolor painter. Through this serendipitous meeting, Sheets's India experience took on a new dimension.

As the aide who so admired Sheets's work was responsible for the viceroy's guest list, the artist was included in many of the viceroy's social events, and through them came to know several influential people. When Lord Lithingow was replaced by Lord Wavell, Sheets continued to be invited to the viceroy's palace.

By the time Wavell arrived in India, over one million people had died in the famine. Hoarding was

Correspondent-artist Millard Sheets: India, December 1943.

widespread and inflation spiraled to new heights. Civil unrest was endemic; Gandhi urged the British to leave India. Wavell was forced to commit fifty-seven infantry battalions to restore order in the countryside and troop morale was low.

At the viceroy's palace, Lady Wavell arranged an exhibit of the work of war artists, in which Sheets was included, among the French, British, and other Americans. He entered his famine paintings. When he and Lady Wavell attended the opening, they found Sheets's work in a closed-off room. Lady Wavell inspected them and then ordered the exhibition closed so that Sheets's work could be properly hung in the main area.

Political and civil unrest motivated the isolation of Sheets's work, and low troop morale inspired Lord Wavell and Lord Mountbatten to plan an offensive. They directed their attention to the Arakan, the coastal region of Burma, near India's Bengal Province. The immediate objective was to capture the Japanese-held Akab Island.

The Allied brigades went into a meat-grinder, as the same military mistakes were repeated time and time again. More than 2,500 men were dead, missing, or wounded, and army morale sank to its lowest level.

Because the situation was so bleak, the thirty-four C-B-I correspondents were tied down in Delhi. The British would not allow them to go to the front; frustration and anger were rampant.

At one of the viceroy's dinners during this time, Sheets sat next to Mountbatten, who had just arrived that evening, and the conversation turned to Sheets's assignment. When the supreme commander of the Allies' Far East theater asked the artist if he was getting what he needed, Sheets's reply was an emphatic,

"No." He told Lord Mountbatten that far from being allowed to go to the front, he had been restricted to Delhi.

Mountbatten took immediate steps to remedy the situation. He arranged for Sheets to fly to the Arakan front where he would accompany Tony Beauchamp, a British documentary cameraman. Almost before he knew it, Sheets was in the jungles of Burma in the middle of deadly combat, both aerial and ground-level.

The worst battle Sheets experienced was Bamboo Hill. The allies had tried unsuccessfully for three years to recapture it from the Japanese. Now a major assault was planned, and Sheets and Beauchamp arranged to be right in the middle of it.

The men bribed a sentry to allow them across the front line. They stopped in the tall grass and waited under a canopy of artillery fire for the morning and the tank force. At dawn, they felt the ground rumble; they jumped into the jeep and quickly slid in close behind the first tank. Beauchamp had his crank-type movie camera running.

The tank commander opened the turret and climbed out to survey the scene with his binoculars. Just then, an echelon of Allied bombers released its cargo, a heartbeat too late. Sheets saw the bombs coming and knew there was no way he could avoid them.

The initial explosive struck about 125 feet in front of the tank and went back for about three miles. The tank commander was decapitated and the villagers, who had been moved three miles from the front for safety, disappeared in an explosion of earth releasing a shower of truncated limbs.

Sheets and Beauchamp were saved by the bulk of the tank. As soon as the commander's body was removed, the lead tank progressed, the men in their jeep

WOMEN AND CHILDREN   *charcoal   10 x 18½ inches   1943*

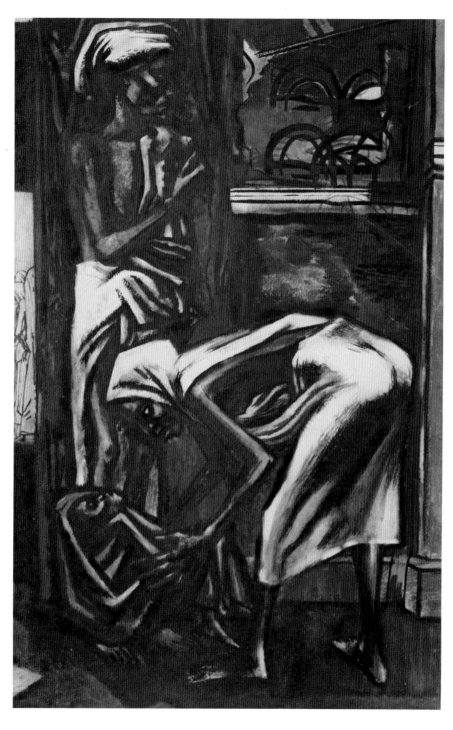

HOUSE OF FAMINE
gouache   31 x 48 inches   1944

right behind. About 200–300 feet ahead, they made a quick left turn and parked behind a hill. They left the jeep and slithered up the incline, where Beauchamp stood up and began panning the area. That action naturally drew fire, and Sheets found himself progressing rapidly down the hill, body pressed tight to the earth. This experience was repeated several times as Beauchamp insisted on getting "one more shot." After six hours, they were close enough to the jeep to make a run for it, back to relative safety, down a narrow jungle trail. "It was enough to cure me for all time of the idea of war."

During the remaining months of Sheets's time in India, he had many more opportunities to feel the brush of death, but somehow he was always spared. Because he had been allowed to go where other correspondents were denied, Sheets provided information for them as well as fulfilling his own role for *Life*. The British heavily censored the work of the political correspondents, and major news, such as General Joseph Stilwell's impending demotion, or possible firing, was not made available to the American people.

In late spring of 1944, Sheets prevailed upon Lord Mountbatten to allow him to leave the area and return home for a rest. Mountbatten acquiesced, and Sheets received his orders to fly back to America. Before leaving, he spent hours with the correspondents as they readied their story on the situation in the C-B-I theater; when he flew from the area, the story was in his case.

The trip back to America was as hazardous as the trip to India had been. After a series of landings and departures at various points of the compass, Sheets arrived in New York, where Mary met him.

Sheets had planned to return to India, but after attending a luncheon hosted by Henry Luce and reporting on what was happening in India and China, he was sent home to California and admonished to "get a rest." No one on the *Time-Life* staff believed the message he brought them from the correspondents.

The story ultimately broke two weeks later and Sheets resigned his commission and finished his projects for *Life*. The armistice was signed just as the printing plates with Sheets's paintings of battle scenes started to roll, and that news changed the entire issue. Sheets's war paintings were never printed, although several articles did appear with his work. "It was an exciting experience, but I was glad when it was over."

Much of the art that Sheets produced during the war—over 100 sketches—is now in the Department of Defense archives, mute testimony to the horror and bitterness he experienced.

This bitterness was also reflected in Sheets's postwar art. His work of this period is dark, the faces angular and tragic. The golden innocence of southern California was gone, lost in the jungles and battlefields of Indo-China and the streets of death in India. The imprint the war had made would not fade. During the mind-numbing events of World War II in the Pacific, Sheets had gone through an emotional and creative catharsis and had deepened his artistic conscience. The sunshine of California and the dark night of death in India combined in Sheets's mind and emotions, and the result was art with more depth and compassion than he had been able to reach before. His energies and drive had been redirected and redefined.

It was September 1945 before Sheets was able to completely end his wartime activities and return to civilian life. When he did, he found that he could not escape the images he had lived with for those months in India. Never before had he seen such utter disregard for the lives of others, such human suffering, such unspeakable atrocities. He had seen remarkable courage on the one hand, violence and cowardice on the other, and whatever was left of glory.

Something of this change in attitude came through in the letters he wrote home to his family. Even before he returned home, he had resolved never to be content with his former way of life. Life seemed to have a deeper meaning. The future that beckoned him would be approached with a far deeper sense of values.

Sheets found that he wanted to do something that would better the world and improve the quality of life for everyone. However, he did want to remain within the world he knew best, art. Teaching, which had been a major part of his life and an activity he had practiced over the years, continued to be a meaningful and important facet of his existence. Still, it seemed to him that he could educate in many ways, both in and out of the classroom.

Soon after his return to California, Sheets had an opportunity to follow through on his theory. He had been directing the art shows at the annual Los Angeles County Fair since the death of his former mentor, Theodore B. Modra; he continued to carry on the latter's tone with shows of California artists and craftsmen. Now, as a director with a new sense of maturity and awareness, he wanted to take the show far beyond local, even national boundaries. He had before him the opportunity, through art, to open people's eyes to the wider world and he was determined to make the most of it.

Sheets gathered together an enthusiastic crew of workers. He selected as his chief assistant Richard Petterson, a fine ceramist who had been born and educated in China and who had a vast knowledge of many crafts. Art critic Arthur Millier was commissioned to write the brochures for the shows.

Several exhibits of much better-than-average quality followed in quick succession. In 1950, the county fair show acquired real impact when the exhibit entitled *Masterpieces of Art from 1790 to 1950* took shape. The show illustrated, through a carefully chosen series of masterworks, the continuity of Occidental art from the time of the French Revolution to the then present day. Attendance soared to 900,000 and from this success, Sheets's epic exhibit, *One World of Art,* evolved.

To justify a title of such breadth, and to conform to the ambitious scale of his idea, Sheets devoted a great amount of planning and work. No show of this scope had ever been attempted by a county fair. To make it sufficiently impressive would require works of both ancient and contemporary artists.

The artist felt that a world so muddled and rife with hatred and fear—all the feeling produced by war—needed an exhibition demonstrating the rich cultural heritage of the former enemies, Germany, Italy, and Japan, as well as that of the former Allies.

Not everyone agreed with him, and he had to convince the board of directors of the fair to give him the opportunity—and the budget—to achieve his vision. A thoughtful planner, Sheets left no loopholes, and the eventual decision was favorable.

Sheets also was able to persuade personal friends at the Metropolitan Museum of Art and other institutions across the country that it would be worthwhile for them to loan pieces from their collections. He was also able to borrow from the Louvre in France and from the British Museum.

The preview of the exhibit was picketed, but not for long. Angry articles were written in the local newspapers about the county fair displaying art from America's former enemies. The furor eventually waned, particularly after the governor of California, Earl Warren, conducted a televised walk-through with Sheets when CBS produced a one-hour television program about the art show.

Throughout all of the praise and criticism, Sheets held firm to the advice of his former mentor, Theodore Modra, who said, "Bring art to the people," which had been Modra's primary concern while he was director of the shows.

To ensure maximum information for the average viewer, Sheets worked out a series of placards, decorated with the appropriate flag for each country represented. On the placard was a brief discussion of the particular nation's contribution to the long history of art and world culture.

Over a million visitors attended the exhibit and Sheets accomplished part of his postwar dream. He had shown his part of the world that art was a universal element, common to the lives of all people and important in its own right, regardless of the sins and excesses of governments.

Following the success of this show, Sheets mounted other trail-blazing exhibits. *Six Thousand Years of Art in Clay* was assembled from such museums as the Louvre, the British Museum, and the Metropolitan in New York City. *Painting in the United States* showcased outstanding American painters from the 1700s to the 1950s. In 1954, *The Arts of Daily Living* demonstrated the myriad possibilities for incorporating taste and design into homes through the technique of self-contained rooms, designed and decorated for maximum effect; this show was produced in collaboration with the magazine *House Beautiful* and was featured in the October issue. The final show mounted under Sheets's direction was in 1955 and entitled *The Arts of Western Living,* which concentrated on the region's unique aspects and the ways in which they could be incorporated into home design.

Eventually, Sheets's postwar work with the Los Angeles County Fair Art Show ended, but the effect of his examples carried on. He persisted in his desire to beautify and educate the world, or at least his portion of it. Sheets followed Modra's philosophy and expanded upon it, often brilliantly, in all of his creative activities.

MORNING AFTER THE RAIN, CENTRAL PARK   *watercolor*   *21 x 29 inches*   *1981*

VARIATIONS ON A THEME: TEACHER

GREAT TEACHERS ARE ONE OF LIFE'S FINEST gifts. They inspire vision and direct individuals into unfamiliar and challenging avenues of learning. Many people are fortunate to have experienced at least one of these individuals; some have had several. Sheets himself had more than his share of extraordinary teachers.

It was partially with the memory of these people, as well as circumstances and inclination, that Sheets began to teach. One of the first to recognize his abilities in this area was Nelbert Chouinard; the realization came to her as she saw many of her own students, some of them years older than Sheets, listen attentively as he discussed their paintings with them. He was without experience, had no teaching credentials, yet in 1927, in his second year as a student in her school, she hired him to teach watercolor painting. This early experience gave him a base for the teaching he was to do in the years to come: first in Claremont, California, at Scripps College, where he remained, in-termittently, for twenty-eight years, and then, during the fifties, as the director of the Otis Art Institute for five years. In addition, it laid the groundwork for the painting workshops he has conducted for many years.

Given Sheets's philosophy on the importance of art in everyone's life, it is not surprising that teaching became one of his abiding passions. It was a vehicle for him to share the joy he personally derived from art as well as to help develop the talents of others so that they could carry the torch. In a sense, everything that Millard Sheets has done with his talent was educational. His art opened people's eyes to new ways of looking at the world and some of its inequities (e.g., *Tenement Flats, Famine in India*) as well as the beauty it contains (e.g., *Golden Hills, Moorea, Monument Valley*). His work as an architectural designer certainly improved the man-made environment, as did the huge wall murals he created. Teaching, then, was another facet of the same jewel.

Sheets's initial contact with Scripps College came

in 1932 when the art department there mounted a show of his paintings. Shortly thereafter, the head of the art department, Morgan Padelford, called him and asked him to meet with Ernest Jacqua, president of the college, to discuss a mural. Sheets met with Jacqua and negotiations had scarcely been concluded when Jacqua contacted him once again and asked him if he would consider teaching at Scripps for a semester while Padelford was in Europe.

Sheets considered this one of the greatest challenges ever put to him. He had no college degree and was but a few years older than most of the people he would be teaching. "But I didn't know enough to be frightened and I loved to teach. I enjoyed being with young people." He was twenty-five at the time.

The facilities for teaching art at Scripps were not the best. Only regular classrooms were provided; they lacked proper lighting for art instruction and were overcrowded. Despite these handicaps, it was an exciting year with many marvelous students. Two of the most exceptional were Milford Zornes and Tom Craig, both of whom went on to become accomplished professional artists.

Sheets's first semester at Scripps was so successful that he was asked to stay on. Partly as a result of his enthusiastic teaching, the art department had grown and both he and Padelford were needed to handle the drawing and painting classes. Within four years, at age twenty-nine, Sheets was made head of the department.

In his first year at Scripps, Sheets repeatedly heard the name of Hartley Burr Alexander. He was spoken of with such awe and reverence that Sheets's curiosity was piqued, as was his ego. Alexander, Scripps's Professor of Philosophy, was well known for his accomplishments in assisting architects and artists in the creation of many buildings, such as the Nebraska State Capitol facility.

When Alexander returned to Scripps, Sheets had the opportunity to meet this paragon of intellect. He found Alexander, who had spent the previous year deciding upon the art and artists for the new Radio City Music Hall in New York, very much like other professors, that is, until he heard him speak. Then he realized why Alexander was so highly regarded by all who knew him.

Later in the semester, Millard and Mary Sheets invited several of his fellow faculty members to dinner at their new home; Alexander and his wife, Nellie, were among the guests. After an excellent meal, at which the wine flowed freely, Sheets began to air some of his complaints about formal education, particularly his belief that the liberal arts college was not very well organized for art students. He felt that some of his especially talented students should be permitted to spend more time in art classes and to devote less study time to the humanities.

Sheets recalls a moment of painful silence after his complaint. "It wasn't painful to me; I was so pontifical at that moment. There is no one as smart as a second-year art student or first-year college instructor."

It was in response to this that Alexander gave Sheets his first real piece of philosophy to ponder. "The trouble with you artists is that you're not educated." Nellie immediately reminded Hartley of his eight o'clock lecture the following morning, and the couple left.

Sheets thought about Alexander's comment most of the night. As he lay awake in the dark room, he began to doubt things he had always felt to be absolutes. Perhaps Alexander was right.

The next morning, Sheets waited for the older man near his office. At seven-thirty, he heard Alexander approaching. Sheets confronted him with the doubts his remarks had generated. "But how exactly does an artist go about getting an education?"

Alexander's response surprised Sheets. There was a moment of silence and then tears glistened in the philosopher's eyes. He invited the young man into his office, then called and cancelled all of his classes for the day. Instead, he and Sheets spent the balance of the time talking. He told Sheets what in his view an educated person really was and why an artist should be well rounded, not just a craftsman. He spoke of the need for a sense of direction, for purpose. This fascinated Sheets, who asked if they could continue the discussion on a regular basis. For the next six years, Sheets went to Alexander's house one evening a week during the school year and they explored the questions Sheets had originally raised at half past seven on that morning in the hall outside their offices. Before long, other artists accompanied Sheets in his weekly seminar; Sheets felt that others should share some of Alexander's wisdom.

It came as a great surprise to Sheets that Alexander, while extremely informed on a wide range of subjects—anthropology; archeology; politics; religion; the arts of Egypt, Greece, and Rome; and Renaissance and seventeenth-century Dutch paintings—had not become deeply involved with the modern world.

Sheets invited Alexander and his wife to accompany him and Mary to an exhibit of one hundred paintings and one hundred drawings by van Gogh,

on display in San Francisco. Alexander was stunned when he saw the exhibition. "Who is this man," he asked Sheets, who replied, "A post-impressionist who painted from his gut."

The four continued to examine van Gogh's art. Suddenly, they realized that Alexander was no longer with them. Worried because he had a history of heart problems, they began to search for him. It was Sheets who finally located Alexander sitting quietly, outside near a fountain. When asked what he was doing, Alexander replied, "Thinking about van Gogh's art—the greatest autobiography ever written." After further contemplation, Alexander authored a work on van Gogh entitled *The Journey of a Man From Darkness into Light,* a reflection of the depths of feeling the artist's work touched in him.

As a teacher, Sheets is credited again and again with an ability to make others believe in themselves, to encourage talent and direct it into productive channels. An example of this ability can be found in the experience of Emil Kosa, Jr. Sheets first encountered Kosa, who was destined to become one of the major artists of California landscapes, at an art exhibit. Sheets was excited by Kosa's work and urged him to submit something to the next county fair art show. One of the pieces Kosa entered was awarded first prize, and Kosa's self-confidence soared. But more than that, Kosa later said, Sheets "resolved my Paris-induced bewilderment about art. 'You know how to paint,' he told me. 'Paint to express yourself.' "

During his first year at Scripps College, Sheets took much the same attitude inside the classroom. He did find it difficult, however, to teach students when the facilities were so poor. Approaching the president of the college about a new studio, he was told that the budget would not allow the type of facility he desired. Sheets proposed a substitute in the form of all-purpose "barn," tucked in a small olive grove on the campus grounds. Jacqua countered with a suggestion of his own; he challenged Sheets to create a Scripps College Fine Arts Foundation and to support its construction through memberships. If a series of exciting exhibits could be arranged, and good speakers hired, he told Sheets, it was likely that Sheets could get what he wanted without asking anyone outright.

Sheets was not enthusiastic about the plan, but a challenge was a challenge. As he began to work on the idea, he became caught up in the possibilities. The first speaker he contacted accepted his offer without a pause. Irving Stone, author of the moving book *Lust for Life,* asked only for a small honorarium of forty dollars, to which Sheets gladly acceded.

One of the patrons of the foundation was Mrs. Josephine Everett, an enthusiastic collector of the work of California artists. She had, in fact, purchased Sheets's painting, *Women of Cartagena,* that had been accepted at the Carnegie International Exhibit. She opened her home to Sheets for a showing of his own paintings and asked him to speak to a group of friends there about the future of art at Scripps College.

In the audience was Mrs. Everett's house guest, Florence Rand Lang, from New Jersey. She was sufficiently impressed by his concepts that afterward she questioned him more closely. The next day, she came to Scripps and toured the facilities and found herself in agreement with him on their inadequacies.

Before he knew what was happening, Mrs. Lang asked him the construction cost for an art building, and upon hearing Sheets's quick estimate of $37,500, said she would send it as soon as she returned to her home in New Jersey. Despite some skepticism on President Jacqua's part, Mrs. Lang followed through, and the money was used to raise a new art instruction building. Several years went by with no word from his benefactress, even though Sheets had had a handsome album made up and sent to her upon the building's completion. Then, just as she had done before, she appeared one day in the large studio where Sheets was teaching. Looking around the crowded room, she remarked that she supposed it was time for a second unit; what did Sheets think it would cost this time? In anticipation of future development, master plans for the whole art building complex had been prepared, and he told her that $180,000 could build the second unit. She acquiesced once again. Three years later, she offered to match, dollar for dollar, Scripps's fund-raising efforts for a third building. The Fine Arts Foundation rallied to the cause, and the members voluntarily gave the money within three weeks. The third building was successfully completed.

These facilities, while beautiful, were for and always secondary to the students. Sheets is particularly proud of two: David Scott and Douglas McClellan. Scott was a fine painter and an excellent art historian. After finishing at Scripps, he went to Harvard and received his doctorate, returning to Scripps as a teacher and later, head of the art department. From there he went to the Smithsonian Institution as an assistant director of American art, then became its director. Today he is on the staff of the National Museum

OLD COLONIAL BRIDGE, MEXICO   *watercolor   22 x 30 inches   1981*

of American Art in Washington, D.C., as planning director. Scott remembers:

Millard in Claremont and Los Angeles in the thirties was surely the right man in the right place at the right time. His creative drive broadened the scope of Scripps College's pioneering humanities curriculum, and the studio complex he built there eventually housed an arts program which made it a regional center with a national reputation. Painters, designers, sculptors and craftsmen came and stayed to form a unique community or left to work, teach, and share the insights acquired in Claremont.

McClellan came to Scripps right after World War II. He had received a year of training at the Colorado Springs School of Art and then, financed by the G.I. Bill, studied with Sheets. He continued his studies in Claremont and received his Master of Fine Arts degree from Claremont Graduate School. After Scott had left the director's position, McClellan took over at Scripps. Today he is head of the art department at the University of California at Santa Cruz.

Not all of Sheets's students came from the academic community. Some, like Jack Zajac, contacted him directly and asked for his help. A sixteen-year-old steel mill worker at the time, Zajac showed Sheets his work: enormous canvasses imbued with terrifically intense feeling. The subjects were codes of bad painting, Sheets recalls, but the talent was definitely there. Zajac did not attend classes regularly—classes for which Sheets quietly paid his tuition—but he was given a work room with another student. It was here that he created the material that won him the Prix de

Rome. Zajac studied sculpture with Bert Stewart and painting with Sheets. However, they served not only as teachers but as guides as well. In Sheets's estimation, Zajac was complete in himself. He never fought his instructors' suggestions—he just did not pay a great deal of attention to them. The primary lesson they taught him was the importance of discipline in the creation of any kind of art, sculpture, or painting.

Another talented student Sheets had at Scripps was Susan Lautmann, later to become Mrs. Carl Hertel. She completed Scripps with honors in art and poetry as well as highest scholarship; later, after graduation, she worked with Sheets for thirty years as his chief assistant in mural execution.

It is students such as these, Sheets feels, who make teaching so rewarding. The transmission of knowledge and the joy of seeing those whom he has worked with go on to achieve prominence is a source of great excitement for Sheets. It is, in a way, a surmounting of the greatest challenge: to spark and set free a questing mind, an incubating talent.

Sheets practiced the self-discipline he so diligently taught others, and helped produce an art department that was the envy and inspiration of many other institutions. He had built it into an influential, lively center for the arts.

The city of Claremont had been awakened by the college's activities and by Sheets's accomplishments. These achievements were recognized in a May 1939 issue of a local newspaper, which praised the school's art department, "so admirably designed for the instruction of students."

In 1953, in the midst of his tenure at Scripps College, Sheets was presented with the type of challenge he handles so well. The Los Angeles County Art Institute, which had been in existence for sixty or more years, had reached the disaster point. There were no academic standards, no criteria of competency among staff members, no discipline, and no philosophy: a damning set of negatives. Further, many of the students had been in attendance for inordinate periods of time; they were professionals at attending classes, not at creating art. The county's board of supervisors realized something had to be done and they turned to Sheets to help them decide what the answers to these problems would be. John Anson Ford, a member of the Los Angeles County Board of Supervisors, spoke with Sheets who was, at the time, recuperating from a riding injury. Sheets told Ford that a publicly supported institution should perform exceptionally well if it is to justify the expenditure of public money, and that the institute as it then existed definitely did not fulfill its goal. An entirely new concept was needed. Ford prevailed upon Sheets to write this concept and Sheets did so. The final product of his thoughts emphasized professional art training combined with a sound liberal arts background.

This stringent idea for upgrading the institute was presented to the full board by Sheets at the California Club. They were also told that new buildings and a more generous budget were necessary if the school was expected to be worthy of public support.

To Sheets's surprise, the board agreed; they went even further and offered him the job of directing this renaissance. After initial reservations, he accepted. He asked for and was granted a leave of absence from Scripps and took up the herculean task that had been presented to him.

He moved in and immediately slashed away the deadwood on the faculty and in the student population. The casualties were high: a majority of the faculty and ninety-five percent of the students were removed. It took Sheets a full year to hire a new faculty and to redesign the school so it would reach the projected standards. He evaluated each job carefully and went after the best people he could find.

The first group of teachers included painter Richard Haines, Italian-born sculptor Renzo Fenci, and ceramist Peter Voulkos. Design would be taught by Leonard Edmondson and drawing by Herb Jepson. Joe Mugnaini was later added to the roster as head of the drawing division. Sheets was also able to attract mosaicist Arthur Ames and ceramist Helen Watson, new head of the ceramic department, as well as Ernest Freed, head of print making.

After three years with a new program, a new faculty, and a new building, the school, now known as Otis Art Institute, came into its own as one of the country's better art schools. It was completely accredited by the Association of Colleges and a whole new aura of competency and energy abounded, infused by Sheets's direction. After six years of building the program, Sheets retired. The school had a somewhat rocky period afterward; in the end, after convoluted machinations by some members of the board of supervisors to the contrary, the Otis Art Institute became part of the New York-based Parsons school of fine art. Sheets's contribution was the buoy by which the Los Angeles County Art Institute escaped the ignominy of closure.

❧

Over the years, Scripps was generous with Sheets in

other ways. The college allowed him three to eight weeks each year to lecture by invitation at colleges in the southern, midwestern, and eastern states in connection with the Association of American Colleges. The theme he always presented was the place of art in daily life and the importance of learning its language as entrée to a fascinating new world.

Sheets traveled to the Universities of Hawaii, New Mexico, and Minnesota, and to the art departments of several southern black colleges, among other places, all the while reveling in the opportunity to repay in some small way what had been so graciously and freely given to him earlier in his career. These experiences offered Sheets a chance to share his knowledge with students from diverse backgrounds, often engaging in a one-on-one dialogue.

It was during one of his lecture trips, this time to the University of Iowa, that he was able to meet Grant Wood. Wood invited Sheets to be his houseguest when he learned that the Californian was to be appearing at the university. When Sheets arrived, he found that Wood was in the hospital, but had insisted that Sheets stay nonetheless. His reception was gracious, and he had an opportunity to talk several times with the famous Iowa painter.

Sheets spent ten years, between 1938 and 1948, traveling across America, visiting colleges and universities, both for the American Colleges program and by invitation, lending vocal and enthusiastic support to his creed: art as a major component of everyone's daily life.

Later, he was invited to officially participate in a government-sponsored lecture and cultural exchange program and to present his message internationally.

The American Specialist Program, initiated by the United States Department of State in the early 1960s, offered Sheets an opportunity to extend his gift for lecturing and teaching into a wider field, while at the same time helping promote American good-will abroad. This program differed from the cultural exchanges that had been going on for several years: people who were involved in similar activities—artists, writers, etc.—were given a chance both to learn from their counterparts in other countries and to disseminate their own country's ideas within a more relaxed forum.

Sheets's first assignment came in 1960, when he was sent to Turkey; he and his wife arrived in the midst of a very cold winter. Sheets had to underwrite Mary's expenses because the State Department was adamant that it would not finance family members. His reasons for including Mary were both practical and personal: he foresaw that her presence would be his entrée into areas that would otherwise be closed to a single man; and since she had been home-bound with their small children during his earlier years of travel, he particularly wanted to have her with him now that the children were grown.

His prediction was borne out, as the couple was invited to private homes and family gatherings where he would have been out of place had he been alone. Mary's enthusiasm was also a plus. "She was a credit to our country—her gentle curiosity and openness to new situations and her sensitivity were extremely important and positive factors in really getting to know a foreign culture."

The couple's stay in Turkey began in Istanbul. Sheets lectured on architectural design and painting and met with university officials. While he gave two or three demonstrations, he found he could not paint

TURKEY *sketch* 1975

effectively. The bitter cold and his unfamiliarity with the situation inhibited his desire to create, but not his willingness to investigate Turkey's many attractions.

As part of Sheets's travels through this ancient land, he saw a twelfth-century example of what he had always tried to accomplish in his own work: the incorporation of aesthetics into buildings to improve the attitudes of those who occupied them. The facility, constructed for the treatment of the mentally disturbed, incorporated water fountains and trickling streams in beautiful open courtyards. Still in use in the twentieth century, the hospital's concept continued to be valid; doctors maintained that the patients were positively influenced by the beauty of their surroundings.

The Sheetses were assisted throughout the trip by an American-educated interpreter, Nigül Matters. She accompanied them on their wanderings about the Turkish countryside and to university and official lectures that Millard Sheets gave. Matters was the link between his English presentation and his audience. Her aid also enabled them to better understand the significance of the museums they explored and the festivals they attended.

After two months in Turkey, and thousands of miles, Sheets and his wife returned to the United States. They had shown the Turks some of America's culture and had absorbed some of the beauty of the Turkish heritage. They had watched camels wrestle and had seen Roman ruins and crusaders' castles, some of which seemed to rise directly from the sea. Sheets had spoken with highly placed officials and common people alike. The experience was such a positive, productive one that the next year, when the State Department suggested that he go the the USSR, he responded eagerly.

Again, Mary accompanied him at his expense. Scheduled to leave in November, they spent a week in Washington, D.C., being briefed prior to their flight. East-West tensions had relaxed momentarily, but it was still a delicate matter for an American to enter Russia, even for so innocuous a mission as that which Sheets was undertaking.

In retrospect, Sheets found that some of the information he was given by the State Department was off the mark. "We were told that we would never be allowed to go where we wanted or be guests in private homes; I was warned that I could not expect to lecture as I had been accustomed to doing; we would never see the same people twice." Nonetheless, Sheets and his wife discovered that, to the contrary, they were given great freedom of movement and welcomed wherever they went. They still fondly recall the warm, human side of the Russians with whom they came in contact, and treasure the memory of this experience.

Sheets took a small Japanese projector and about 800 slides with him on this trip. The subjects illustrated included a historical overview of American architecture and art and a rather complete résumé of his own work on the California landscape—all exotic subjects for his Russian audiences. Sheets and his wife expected some difficulty entering the USSR with this equipment and some objection to their desired itinerary, which included central Asia. It came as a surprise when border officials responded amicably to the contents of their baggage and to their travel requests.

An interpreter, Lydia Moroshkiva, was provided for them, a quick, personable woman who had done extensive work in the translation of British and American plays and books for the Russian stage. Millard and Mary also found, to their delight, that they would not be consigned to the usual tourist hotels but rather were given accommodations in such pleasant hotels as Moscow's Sovietskaya and Leningrad's Astoria.

This time, Sheets had gone prepared to paint. He was encouraged in this activity by his hosts, who provided him with numerous opportunities. They facilitated his trips to Moscow, Leningrad, Armenia, Uzbekistan, Tashkent, Samarkand. Even the biting wind and deep snow of the Russian winter did not deter the couple from their explorations. The magnificent buildings of Moscow's Red Square and Zagorsk's religious center, enshrouded in the snow's blinding purity, proved to be striking subjects.

Sheets gave a total of seventeen lectures while in the USSR; he spoke to enthralled audiences, whose members demanded to see all 800 slides, rather than the 50 or 60 he had planned to show. "They were hungry for information about America. Mary and I visited hundreds of artists' studios and private homes in addition to the more formal lectures I was giving. In every instance, the interest and enthusiasm displayed by these people was just incredible."

Sheets was strongly affected by the situation of Russian artists; they could be endlessly creative but often were not permitted to exhibit. The thought of this hidden, unwitnessed work touched Sheets; that these people shared their work with him was a compliment to his sensitivity.

As Sheets and his wife traveled in the USSR, they were sought out by individuals and government officials and their opinions on the country were solicited. Both Millard and his wife tried to be frank, but courteous, in their responses. The couple was frequently struck, however, by the extent of Soviet propoganda. They most often encountered this while in airport VIP waiting rooms. There they found the *Moscow News,* a digest of articles and editorials from a variety of periodicals, printed in several languages, and, in Sheets's estimation, unfailingly inaccurate and slanted.

When they returned to America two days before Christmas, Sheets went to the State Department for debriefing. His comments on his Russian experiences were typical of his personal, forthright style: "I told them that my initial briefing was almost totally erroneous and that the program itself was extremely valuable, particularly if they would encourage exchange lecturers to take their spouses." Ultimately, Sheets was invited back to Washington, D.C., twice, once to speak to all 2,500 members of the State Depart-

DOMES OF ZAGORSK, RUSSIA *acrylic* *29 x 40 inches* *1980*

ment and again to speak to the American Specialist Program's board of directors.

"I am deeply grateful for the opportunities given to me by this program. It was an important gesture, a significant effort toward establishing positive bonds between countries. This was also an effort to get through to people and to ameliorate some of the frightening differences that are perceived between various nations. The exchange of ideas that happened as a result of the American Specialist Program was a bright spot in an otherwise troubled decade."

Sheets was associated with another well-known southern Californian, Walt Disney, in the planning and direction of a school that was close to Disney's heart: the California Institute of the Arts, or Cal Arts as it came to be known.

In order to produce the vital talent the film industry needed—indeed, consumed with a voracious appetite—Disney conceived of this school as a place where top-flight students could learn the crafts of cinematography, graphic and applied arts, music, drama, and dance from those best qualified to teach them. Disney consulted with Sheets regarding those individuals who would be the most authoritative and talented to teach art; Sheets was happy to be involved in a project of this magnitude.

Before all the arrangements could be solidly established, however, Cal Arts was unceremoniously launched onto center stage with Disney's sudden death in the late 1960s. Roy Disney, Walt's older brother and business associate, became concerned that he might also die before his brother's dream could be realized; as a result, planning for the school was pushed through rapidly and staffing was done, according to Sheets, "with little regard for the clear objectives that Walt

had envisioned." Sheets was invited to serve on the board of directors of Cal Arts, and in deference to Disney's memory, agreed to do so. Eventually, after eight years of service, Sheets submitted his resignation. "I found myself increasingly disturbed by the direction in which the school's leadership was taking it. The art department was approaching the education of its students in the same old *laissez faire* way: 'Bring them in, put them around talented people. It will work out.' The trouble is, in my mind, it does *not* work out." It is always difficult to abandon the dream of a friend, but Sheets felt that the dream was fragmenting, and he could not support the new philosophy, and so, regretfully, he left the board to those who were comfortable with Cal Arts' evolving style of instruction.

Painting workshops provided Sheets with other opportunities to articulate and practice his beliefs. They included all the things Sheets liked to do best—paint, travel, teach, and lecture. A continuation of his teaching career was undertaken in this particularly American phenomenon that has induced countless serious students, amateurs, professional painters, and art lovers to spend their vacations in a pleasant mix of art instruction, travel, and good company.

There are two general types of workshops. The smaller ones are either organized by colleges or other groups who hire the best teachers they can afford, or individuals who conduct their own workshops, one-day sessions of work and demonstration, lectures and critiques. Larger and more sophisticated are the traveling workshops, those that seem to go everywhere in search of picturesque locations. The oldest and most prestigious of these are the Hewitt Painting Workshops, conducted by three enterprising brothers whose close association in business began when they organized lemonade stands as children.

The Hewitt brothers adhere to the practice of selecting good students and they were among the first to offer workshops in many parts of the United States and throughout the world. Doug Kingman was their first teacher, followed by Millard Sheets, Rex Brandt, Tom Hill, George Post, the late Barse Miller, and Robert E. Wood. Sheets joined the Hewitt group in 1963 and his workshops have proven to be extremely popular.

Critiques and discussions are important features of these sessions. Sheets particularly believes in the workshop concept, and sincerely feels that his students learn more than they would in an ordinary class because of the intensity with which instruction is given and received. He sets a good pace and assigns problems that require a great deal of thought. Sheets is aware that most individuals, painting alone, day after day, would not set these types of tasks for themselves. He feels that he also benefits from the sessions and from the students in the intense two or three weeks of concentration. "It's like a dry-cleaning for everyone involved."

The painting workshops have included trips to Guatemala, Mexico, Hong Kong, Hawaii, Italy, Japan, Greece, Yugoslavia, Ireland, and Portugal. In 1982, there was a trip to Alaska (sponsored by the Alaskan Artists' Guild); in 1983, Mexico; and in 1984, it will be India-Nepal. Aside from the lure of travel to glamorous painting sites, what makes Sheets's workshops outstanding is the quality of his instruction and the message he conveys.

A professional, Sheets arrives fully prepared and organized. His manner is attractive, relaxed, and easy,

eager to share his wide experiences with his students. With sincerity and enthusiasm, he explains his vision of the role the artist must play in order to make art an active part of daily living. Like a good actor, he has the ability to put himself and his ideas across.

An education in art reaches far beyond the mastery of techniques, according to Sheets; one must become a total person. The broader the base of general education, the more able the artist is to cope with the environment. Sheets feels that gratitude for life itself is basic to the development of an insight beyond the average.

When artists lose touch with reality, they cannot hope to produce art that will have a practical meaning. The fields of furniture and industrial design, city planning, and architecture have been neglected by the very artists who could most contribute beauty as well as efficient usefulness.

In former times, Sheets reminds his students, artists were trained to produce useful things. The tradesman was an artist-craftsman, the religious artist was subsidized by church patrons who sought graphic representations of beatific concepts. Many of these extraordinarily talented people could neither read nor write; their most effective means of learning was through the medium of art—stained glass windows, tapestries, sculptures. The artist was not an individual starving in the attic but a person trained to express the ideas of his time.

Of the thousands of artists in the United States today, Sheets claims that only a small percentage are able to make their living from fine arts alone. With few exceptions, artists scorn the practical, the useful manifestions of common living. They live apart in a world of their own, and in this limited experience they hope to produce works that the public will understand.

Sheets believes the purpose of the artist is to serve society in the search for reasons to live, rather than to be involved only in egocentric demonstrations of techniques and styles. Art, he teaches, is not peripheral. Artists have exciting opportunities for working in industry, and in architecture. He implores his listeners not to escape to the ivory tower. Even Leonardo da Vinci and Michelangelo had to deal with real people, real situations, and real commitments.

In terms of technique, he tells his students to really learn to draw and to paint, but he never dictates the way they put their ideas on paper. He does not impose his personal tastes on his students, and he directs them not to copy but to make their own statement. Many options exist, many choices with respect to medium, subject, tone, color, design, and purpose in painting. The artist can go from harsh realism to complete abstraction. "We have heard people make remarks like, 'He's a brilliant writer but he really doesn't say anything.' It's the same with painting. I admire cleverness but it's more important to say something. The language of art is among the most exciting of all languages."

Sometimes after he has lectured, Sheets demonstrates his use of watercolor. Working on a heavy, tilted table with a large reflecting mirror suspended over it, he works instinctively using his sense of design and color. He demonstrates the way in which design pulls a composition together and he tells the students that abstract design is the fundamental means of organizing feelings and thoughts within the limits of the paper.

Sheets paints boldly but with conviction in every stroke. As students work on their own watercolors, he circulates around the room, generous in the time he gives to critiques.

Sheets puts strong emphasis on drawing. He urges his students to draw every day, to find out something they did not know the day before, and to grapple with the problems of structure. Drawing is fundamental for disciplining the mind and enhancing dedication. Sheets will often hand each student a flower, or perhaps a weed two inches long, and then tell them to enlarge it to four feet by four feet. "Now you're not drawing a bunch of little tit-tat facts, you're forced to draw structure." Great emphasis is placed on drawing because Sheets feels it is crucial that an artist understand the meaning of structure. "Every artist must have the ability to understand and control . . . what lies behind what is seen with the eye. Drawing with this approach in mind demands that you think less about making a drawing and more about what constitutes the world. The mind needs to comprehend what is behind a subject. It's easy for an artist to become a sad victim of his eye, when he really needs to see with his mind."

Sheets becomes animated when he speaks of teaching. His clear blue eyes sparkle at the potential for new ideas to emerge between teacher and student. He says, "I have learned as much from my students as I hope they have learned from me."

A third part of Sheets's triumvirate of educational activities comes when he functions as part of a jury. An art jury is similar to its courtroom counterpart in that both make judgments on the quality of the material presented to them. Professional artists regard jurying as part of paying their dues, and many art teachers are also included in this group. It is a way of sharing, returning to students that which was given to them early in their own careers. Honorariums in no way compensate for the time and effort put forth by the people who participate in art juries.

In his role as judge, Sheets is very catholic in his tastes. His choices are for fine quality regardless of style, and he is reputed to be very fair in his evaluations.

Sheets always arrives for a jurying session on time and full of vigor, hoping that some of the paintings will show evidence of the inner qualities of the artists. First he looks at the entire array of submissions, familiarizing himself with its variety. He then eliminates the paintings that are obviously not on a level necessary for the exhibit. The remaining entries are separated into the "sures" and the "possibles," and then once again sorted and evaluated. The final selection of work for the show is then made. It is often a painful choice. Many artists paint very well; some, of course, do better work than others, and these are selected for prizes, which are awarded late in the day. The reputation and status the juror acquires for intelligent, fair selections can make or break a show. Sheets's reputation is one of the best. No judgment is hasty, for he is always eager to find work which shows that flash of brilliance, that inner glow of the artist.

In the commission of his duties as a juror, Sheets has gone to all parts of the country and has examined a wide variety of artistic styles. He has been part of art juries for the Carnegie, the American Watercolor Society in New York, and the Metropolitan Museum of Art in New York City as well as countless others. He takes his duties very seriously, and his love for art is reflected in the choices he has made.

THE ASSUMPTION: *a preliminary sketch for the painted mural executed for Our Lady of the Assumption Catholic Church, Ventura, California.*

VARIATIONS ON A THEME: ENTREPRENEUR

MILLARD SHEETS IS A "MAN WHO GETS THINGS done." His natural proclivity for becoming involved in a wide variety of projects has sometimes exhausted him and kept him far from his family, but he has seldom been bored with life.

An artistic entrepreneur, Sheets's firm belief that art has a functional as well as decorative purpose led to the creation of Millard Sheets Designs, Inc., in 1953; at the height of large-project activity, the studio employed between twenty-five and thirty artisans and architects. The success of this venture was fueled by a renewed interest in the marriage of art and architecture that developed in America following the end of World War II. The long-neglected concept of enriching a building with ornamentation had been revived. New techniques, a wide selection of materials, and a multiplicity of forms and textures inspired even the most relentless advocates of sterile and understated design to experiment with restrained color and a modest amount of decoration.

Sheets saw this trend as a tremendous opportunity: the landscape could be beautified and others could be instructed in the possibilities for practical application of artistic theory *vis à vis* the design studio. Although appreciative of the introspective artist who separates himself from the world in order to create, Sheets always identified with those who applied their talent. "It is unfortunate that so many artists seem to resent the necessity of making a living in the real world," he has commented. Sheets's own attitude is a realistic combination of aesthetic sensibility and the need to apply this to buildings, murals, mosaics, and displays, or whatever was required.

To house his studio, which was often reminiscent of a medieval craft guildhall, Sheets and architect David Underwood designed and had built an office building and drafting room with a connecting atelier. On Claremont's Foothill Boulevard, the studio housed this assemblage of talent under one roof. Here, clients, designers, and registered architects cultivated ideas that were passed through the drafting room and into the hands of craftspeople and builders, while in the atelier, artists created mosaics, murals, and sculptured reliefs. Sheets has always received gratification from utilizing the talents of others and showing them how they can be both creative and productive while retaining their independence.

One of Sheets's former students, Susan Hertel, took his message particularly to heart and became not only a pivotal member of his circle of assistants but a valued friend as well. Because of her talent and managerial abilities, Sheets had the freedom to travel during the course of commissions without the additional burden of worrying about projects that were under development in the studio. For thirty years, Hertel worked for Sheets in every phase of the studio's business; in addition, she was almost totally responsible for all the stained glass work produced by Millard Sheets Designs, Inc. She chose the colors, painted the glass, and supervised the installations. After Sheets retired, Susan Hertel became president of the corporation and ran it very effectively. "It would have been impossible for me to do my own work had I not been able to rely so heavily on Sue. She was vital to the studio, and to Mary and me as well."

The working staff also included engineers, registered architects, and draftsmen. They were particularly critical to the success of Sheets's architectural designs, and many innovative forms were brought to fruition through their efforts.

As a designer, Sheets sought to balance the physical requirements of a project with its aesthetic possibilities. During the thirty years in which Sheets divided his time between art and architecture, he created and supervised an enormous number of major

projects. Murals, mosaics, stained glass; private homes, public buildings, office buildings: a prodigious output for one career but especially remarkable when it is considered that during these same years he was also painting and teaching. A voracious appetite for experiences and challenges spurred Sheets on.

Almost two decades of commissioned work preceded the formal establishment of Millard Sheets Designs, Inc. Sheets's reputation began to grow soon after he completed a mural for the Pasadena Young Men's Christian Association in 1929, and thereafter, he was increasingly sought out by firms of wide reputation and distinction.

Houbigant, an internationally known perfume manufacturer, contacted Sheets in 1936. An impressive, eight-window-wide display and an interior sales aisle that could ultimately be taken apart and moved between twenty major American cities was needed, and the Houbigant executives believed that Sheets would provide them with the aura they sought.

Sheets accepted the challenge, in spite of the fact that he was preparing to leave his Claremont home for a teaching assignment in Hawaii and had absolutely no experience in designing such displays. In a matter of days, he had completed a set of plans, drawn to scale and accompanied by specifications and watercolor renderings. These were flown to New York, approved, and returned to Sheets in California with a contract that specified that he must manufacture the displays himself. The first deadline established was two days after his scheduled return from Hawaii.

Undaunted, perhaps exhilarated by the novelty of the project, Sheets contacted his friend, Harold Graham, who was a designer and a very talented engineer. Graham also had a local shop and the necessary

A skilled group of artisans fabricated many of the mosaics, murals, and stained glass ornamentations developed at Millard Sheets Designs, Incorporated.

equipment. Using Sheets's specifications, Graham, William Manker (ceramist), and several other craftsmen fabricated the displays, while Sheets was teaching half an ocean away. The Houbigant contract was successfully fulfilled.

It was not long before Sheets and his associates were producing mechanical window displays for department stores, created in materials such as glass, ceramic, and satin. All designs, preliminary sketches, and working guides came from Sheets, but their execution required the work of many skilled people, men and women solicited by Sheets from among his students and friends.

When Sheets designed buildings, he worked with a variety of architects, and was involved in supervising the construction of buildings and installing their appointments. In most cases, his commission included both the structure and everything that accompanied it: landscaping, sculpture, murals, furniture, wall-coverings, right down to the carpet.

Two of the major projects that Sheets undertook early in his career serve as benchmarks of his reputation as a designer. The air school facilities he created for retired Army Major Corliss C. Moseley and the office building designed for Howard Ahmanson, prominent West Coast financier, set the standards that succeeding projects had to match.

In 1939, on the eve of World War II, Sheets was approached by a friend, Major Corliss C. Moseley, who needed his assistance in executing a job the latter had undertaken for the government. Moseley, a pilot in World War I and operator of a flight training school, had accepted a government commission to plan and supervise the construction of an air school that would be able to train about 900 young men at a time. The luxury of leisurely planning was not available, as the military was concerned with getting as many qualified people into the air as possible. The government therefore turned to private individuals to accomplish the task with alacrity.

Moseley, in response, turned to Sheets for help in finding a contractor. Sheets was able to oblige him with the name of a man, Clarence Stover, who could do the job. While more than willing to undertake the project, Stover pointed out to Moseley that he could not build this large facility (at a cost of $1 million in 1939) from information jotted on the back of an envelope.

It was at this point that Sheets became intimately involved with the air school project. He accepted the commission offered him to design and supervise the construction of a completely functioning facility within a period of about three months. As he later commented, the design was done barely one jump ahead of the contractor.

There were very specific requirements established for these fields; among the most restrictive was that there had to be 25 miles of airspace around each field, and they had to be situated no more than 2,500 feet above sea level. Sheets became familiar with airplane controls and was soon piloting himself across the Southwest in search of suitable locations for the schools.

The first facility, Cal Aero, was completed on schedule in 1940, with a monumental effort from everyone involved. It became the prototype for sixteen more schools built during the next three years, including Thunderbird and Falcon fields in Arizona,

Cal Aero, flight training school built for the United States Government in 1940, was one of Sheets's early large design commissions. Built to process 900 men at a time, Cal Aero was begun in June 1940 and the first cadets entered in August of the same year.

and Fort Stockton and Corsicana in Texas. The last field was finished within months after the Japanese bombed Pearl Harbor.

The second major commission of Sheets's early career came in 1953 when a California financier contacted him about designing a building that would "look good thirty-five or forty years from now, when I'm gone." The project was also a turning point of sorts for the artist; here was his first opportunity to be deeply involved with the building-mural combination that would later become a hallmark of his work.

Howard Ahmanson was a brilliant and eccentric character. He had made a great deal of money through his various business activities, and when he initially contacted Sheets, he was ready to embark on another.

Ahmanson had taken a close look at the com- mercial buildings that lined Wilshire Boulevard in downtown Beverly Hills, California. None of them impressed him. Serendipitously, about this same time, he saw a photograph of the Pacific Clay Products headquarters in the *Los Angeles Times* and was impressed. Ahmanson discovered that Millard Sheets had designed the facility; he contacted the young artist in a fashion typical of his style: he sent Sheets a telegraphically worded letter. Staccato in cadence, it said in part: "Dear Sheets. Saw photograph building you designed, *L.A. Times.* Liked it. I have two valuable properties, Wilshire Boulevard, need buildings. Have driven Wilshire Boulevard twenty-six years, know every building built, names of most architects, bored. . . . Call me."

Sheets, even if he had been so inclined, could not

resist the impulse to speak with this curious man. He called Ahmanson and was invited to lunch at the exclusive Beverly Hills Club the next day. Ahmanson gave him the address of his office and asked Sheets to meet him there, and they would drive to the club together.

When Sheets arrived at the South Spring Street address, he was sure he had made an error. The building was unprepossessing, to say the least. As he ascended to Ahmanson's top floor office via a rickety old elevator, he began to wonder if he had made an error in judgment; this wonder turned to conviction as he found himself in a sea of desks and confusion that made garment-district sweatshops look spacious by comparison.

Sheets's initial impression of Ahmanson was not much more reassuring. In the middle of a poorly lit, sherbet green room, the financier sat with his feet on the desk, speaking rapid-fire into the telephone. After a minimal acknowledgment of Sheets's presence, he resumed his conversation. Then, abruptly, he hung up, reached behind him for his jacket, and told Sheets, "Let's go."

Once settled in Ahmanson's chauffeur-driven Cadillac, the two men began a conversation that carried through lunch and that Sheets still vividly recalls as one of the most exciting of his life; however, the nature of the project never arose. After the extended meal, they began their return trip. As they drove down Wilshire Boulevard, Ahmanson pointed out his lots, but said nothing else about them.

Finally they arrived at the parking lot in back of Ahmanson's office, and here Sheets's curiosity was at least partially satisfied—Ahmanson wanted him to design an office building for one of the lots, and if he liked it, he would commission Sheets to do the second. He gave Sheets explicit instructions regarding the latter's responsibilities: "Design it as though you were doing it for yourself." Beyond this, Ahmanson made it clear, Sheets was not to contact him for anything; he would inspect the structure when it was complete. Sheets was directed to work with other individuals within Ahmanson's organization for details on function, size, and the like.

This unconventional man offered Sheets a challenge that few creative people could resist but that most businesspeople would shudder to accept. The young artist was given full design, supervisory, and financial responsibility and, despite serious misgivings about the whole idea, he undertook the task. The project, he eventually discovered, was a building to house National American Insurance Company offices.

In every other architectural design situation with which Sheets was familiar the art budget had been entirely separate from the main construction budget. In this instance, Sheets did something he had not previously attempted: he incorporated art—mosaics, sculpture, and paintings—into the building's design and the costs for it, directly into the budget. Ahmanson, true to his word, declined to discuss any of this. Sheets was told by Kenneth Childs, one of Ahmanson's primary assistants, to proceed at his own discretion.

Finally, after months of intensive work, the project was ready for Ahmanson's inspection. Sheets, who had taken the financier's orders seriously, had assiduously overseen costs and construction. "I beat everyone down to the lowest costs they could manage; when I was done talking, people felt they were fortunate to be allowed to work on the building."

This office building, which was torn down many

years later to make way for construction of the Ahmanson Center, represented a turning point in Sheets's career. It looked as though it had always been part of the environment; Sheets had directed landscaping with mature trees and shrubs, and had had the raw earth covered with turf. A fountain splashed in the courtyard, and the spacious foyer was adorned with art. A richly detailed mosaic, designed and executed by Sheets, caught the eye of everyone entering.

Ahmanson was delighted, both aesthetically and professionally. While he had not given Sheets any specific guidance—indeed, had probably not known himself precisely what he wanted—the resulting structure was the realization of his only articulated objective: a structure that would "look good" for decades to come.

Ahmanson also observed that the appearance alone would sell quantities of insurance. People could not help but be reassured by the quality and substance of the company's facilities, and that positive feeling would be transferred to the company's product. He gambled on Sheets's ability to design and supervise a large project with essentially no direction beyond his own innate sense of beauty and function. Sheets, on the other hand, risked months of time and effort in pursuit of a concept. He had no assurance Ahmanson would accept what he had done. There was no approval of plans and budget, nor were there site inspections.

The results of mutual trust and respect between the two men were spectacular, and led to a milestone in Sheets's career. He went on to design another structure for Ahmanson's second Wilshire lot, intended to house Home Savings and Loan. It also incorporated substantial amounts of art and elegant appointments; the mural Sheets created for the façade over the lintel was to become intimately identified with Home Savings and Loan. The financier's earlier astute prediction was proven correct; within the first ten days, $19 million in new accounts was generated and as a result, the new banking facility was completely paid for. Ahmanson and Sheets had both taken risks, and the risks paid off. As this financial institution grew, operations and properties were expanded, and Sheets was ultimately instrumental in the design of more than forty Home Savings and Loan buildings.

Perhaps inspired by the success of Ahmanson's Home Savings operations, other financial institutions sought Sheets's talent for their business structures. The fundamental but nebulous qualities of trustworthiness, stability, and character were transformed into mortar and stone, sculpture and mosaic under Sheets's direction. Three Texas financial institutions: the interior of the Mercantile National Bank in Dallas, the Republic Bank in Lubbock, and the Travis Savings and Loan in San Antonio, are representative of Sheets's ability to transform "substance" from an ethereal to a physical state.

As the reputation of the design studio and its founder grew, Sheets's services were sought by an impressive clientele covering a broad spectrum. One of his most dramatic architectural commissions came in 1961, when he was approached by Judge Ellsworth Meyer, who was a Mason and involved with the selection of a designer for the Scottish Rite Temple that the organization planned to build in Los Angeles. Sheets was the only non-Mason interviewed. During the course of their discussions, Sheets posed as many questions as he answered. After a pleasant dinner meeting, he left them with a long list of queries relating to their reasons for wanting a new temple and their expectations of the design. Months went by, and Sheets

Hollywood Home Savings and Loan—an intricate mosaic portrays a parade of famous Hollywood denizens.

(inset) The painstaking detail that goes into any mosaic is evident in this figure of western movie great, Gary Cooper.

As with all Home Savings and Loan facilities, these at Beverly Hills (left) and Palos Verdes, California (right), reflect the use of art as an integral part of the building and site.

began to think he had frightened them off, when Meyer contacted him again; this time the selection committee was prepared to respond.

The second meeting was followed by several others and in the end, the artist's thoroughness and thoughtfulness prevailed. Sheets was commissioned to design the new temple. When he began, he was stunned by the tremendous number of elements that had to be included. The temple represented a type of organizational city, and the auditorium, a crucial gathering place, needed to seat 3,000; there was to be a dining room with seating for 1,500; lodges and recreational areas were other necessities.

Sheets needed to incorporate all these requirements into one aesthetically pleasing building. He also developed mosaics and sculpture as integral parts of the structure. Since the Masons were concerned that their temple symbolize the major concepts of religion and

law, Sheets designed the largest mosaic he had attempted to date. It was to go on the east exterior of the temple, and the subject matter spanned centuries. From King Solomon to twentieth-century California, the mosaic is in the tradition of Gothic religious art, which imparted tradition to those who could not read.

To symbolize the greatness of spirit emphasized by the Masons, Sheets collaborated with sculptor Albert Stewart. Together they designed eight figures representative of the temple builders from Egyptian times through to the twentieth century; the designs were sent to Rome where a skilled craftsman carved them in solid travertine. When completed, they were placed on the south façade. The result of this dramatic adornment is a building on which the traditions and the philosophy of Masonry can be read like a book.

The interior of the temple was not overlooked—murals of all sorts abound. The huge auditorium is enhanced by a symbolic mural depicting the history of the Masons in California; the reading room that is part of the library facility has a mural that is one of Sheets's favorites, a moody representation of ancient trees. More murals decorate the dining room walls.

The Los Angeles Masonic Temple was a complex project and ultimately consumed about four years of Sheets's time. Following its successful completion in 1965, he worked with an architect, a long-time Mason, on the San Francisco Scottish Rite Temple. Though more simple than the Los Angeles facility, it also needed to portray symbolically the meaning and activities of the Masons. The focal piece of the exterior decoration of this temple is a very large grill, with the figures of temple builders worked into it. Mosaic insets in the figures give the grill a particularly striking appearance.

These two projects, large in and of themselves, take on additional significance when included in the whole of Millard Sheets's work. He has often been considered an executive artist, and the Masonic temples typify him at his best in this area. Ultimately responsible for the outcome of these projects, Sheets organized the details, recruited additional artisans as needed, and often personally designed much of the artwork. His technique of inspiring the most creative people to do their best work has been tremendously successful.

The large design projects that Sheets was involved with, such as the Home Savings and Loan buildings and the Masonic temples, are representative of one aspect of the artist's entrepreneurial activity. Regardless of the specific purpose of these structures, Sheets always endeavored to include art as in integral—rather than optional—component. This is entirely consistent with his own personal philosophy that art in some form ought to be part of everyone's daily environment.

He has had the opportunity to enrich that environment through other studio projects as well. While not on as large a scale as buildings, this wide variety of commissioned work often displays Sheets's design and creative force at its best.

Murals, those captivating forms of expression that Sheets first encountered while at Chouinard, constitute a large part of his commissioned work. Many impressive mosaic and painted murals have been developed by the artist; he has always taken particular delight in their creation. His work in this area falls well within a very ancient tradition; wall decoration has been intimately associated with architecture since earliest recorded time. The challenges of working on such large scale have always seemed to intrigue Sheets. He constantly experimented with ways of dealing with the three major dictums of mural design—appropriateness of subject, integration of the mural into the larger architectural scheme, and effective use of symbolism (which requires the most simple terms of expression)—and the results were impressive.

The melding of Sheets's creativity and organizational acumen, plus his talent for acquiring and inspiring the best talent available to him, has resulted in many notable works. Spanning more than thirty-five years, Sheets's activities in this area have resulted in over 150 murals, produced in a variety of media: oil, acrylic, mosaic, stained glass, and carved wood. Regardless of the medium, they all exhibit the artist's propensity to create using flowing line and vibrant

Winner of the 1962 National Academy of Design's Edward Austin Abbey competition, this mural reflects Sheets's concept of the library as a repository for the best of mankind's ideas.

color. He translates his style rather than changing it.

Among the first very large commissions that the design studio was responsible for executing "in house" was the 60-by-22-foot mural that currently resides under the portico of the Detroit Public Library. Sheets and his staff fabricated this mosaic mural and installed it as well.

The commission resulted from Sheets winning the New York National Academy of Design's Abbey competition. This prize, endowed by the late nineteenth-century muralist Edward Austin Abbey, was awarded to a member of the academy by a jury made up primarily of architects and painters. The Abbey fund financed the winner's work, which was then given as a gift to an appropriate organization or community. In 1962, the commission was selected for the Detroit Public Library, which had just added an entrance to its new wing.

No thematic restrictions were placed upon the nine competitors. All of them submitted designs, and all who entered were reimbursed for their work, with the exception of the artist finally chosen by the academy's jury. In that case, the sum was applied toward the total job cost.

Sheets selected as an organizational motif the concept that ideas flow like a river, and libraries house the best of these ideas. He used very large symbolic figures in the center and on two sides, with smaller figures tying them all together. Interesting detail was included; as a result the finished piece reads well both from a distance and up close. This is not always the case with large murals, because when the scale doubles, for example, from six to twelve feet, problems of proportion also multiply rather than diminish. To achieve simplicity and power in the forms required concentration and care.

The combination of a well-conceived design and the opportunity to create that design at the studio itself resulted in a project with which Sheets is still pleased.

The library tower mural at the University of Notre Dame in Indiana is another of Sheets's most widely known creations. He initially was contacted by a group of Minneapolis architects, Ellerbe and Associates, with whom he had been involved when he fashioned a mural for the diagnostic center of the Mayo Clinic in 1953. In this project, a "library of mural painting" according to Sheets, each floor of the clinic had a special work created by an international cast of artists,

Sheets among them. Pleased with his work, in 1963 the architects submitted his name to the Notre Dame officials, along with a dozen others.

Ellerbe and Associates assisted the university in its efforts to rebuild and reorient the campus, a major institutional shift. The library occupied one end of the new campus axis, and the tower dominated the building. The mural was to cover the central part of the tower, a horizontal span of 68 feet, and extend straight up from the entrance door to the top, approximately 134 feet. Even disregarding the creative challenge posed by this size, the mechanics involved were substantial.

The engineers were adamant that granite was the only feasible material for a mosaic mural. The extremes of heat and cold that mark the climate in South Bend, Indiana, dictated this material, stressed one particularly vehement man. This opinion influenced Sheets, and he investigated potential colors and textures with which he could expect to design the mural. He put to work friends and stone brokers around the world, searching out unusual tones of granite; eventually the tally of colors reached an amazing 143 shades.

After discussing the mechanics of the design with the architects, the artist met with Father Theodore M. Hesburgh and his assistant, Father Edmund P. Joyce, to achieve some understanding of the concept they sought to express. To his surprise, they turned the whole responsibility back to him. They expressed their faith in his abilities and, after a long day's discussion, suggested that he submit two or three variations for their group's consideration.

Of the three sketches finally submitted, the second was chosen. The first design was quite representational, with a full-length figure of Christ standing on a rock with the multitude below. The third variation was much more abstract: a tree shape, its limb-like forms supporting groups of scholars. In retrospect, Sheets feels that this idea would have been too static to be really successful, although it was architecturally interesting.

The second design immediately struck the study group as the best. The figure of Christ, arms extended, is cut by a flow of figures representing the disciples and other people of ancient wisdom. Christ's lower body disappears down into the processional. The main figure, with its accompanying swirl of forms, echoes the startling upthrust of the tower itself.

The preliminary work took over a year to finish—a complete, detailed design was made and granite colors were selected. Sheets located a space large enough to allow him to lay out the 134-by-68-foot mural on one gigantic strip of paper. In order to ensure that the corners would be perfectly square, a surveyor's glass and tripod were used. Once the boundaries were established, the pattern was divided into a grid with squares measuring 10 by 10 feet. This precision was important both because of the extremely large size of the project and its design. Composed of very powerful diagonal and vertical lines, the effect of the mural could have been ruined by any inaccuracy.

The specific colors and their delineation on the mural were then indicated on the gridwork pattern; finally, the entire strip was divided into smaller strips that measured 68 horizontal feet by 10 vertical feet. After final checks were made of the granite colors and textures, and the grids were reviewed for accuracy, the first strip was shipped to Cold Spring, Minnesota, where master stone craftsmen would work from the pattern to fabricate the project in sections.

Sheets and his assistants watched with some trepidation as the strips left for Cold Spring; there was no room for error or momentary loss of concentration in what they had done. Once established, colors could not be altered—they had to be absolutely right, color against color. This was the largest space Sheets had ever attempted to cover with a mural, and the challenge it presented had its oppressive side.

Throughout the planning and execution of this mural, Sheets worried that something might not be transferred to the stone as he had envisioned it. However, since the proportions were so great, there was no convenient way he could see the sections assembled before they were put up on the library tower. In the end, this problem was overcome by the artist's determination: he rented bleachers, had large plywood sections laid against them at an angle, and then prepared to climb the highest structure in the vicinity, a ninety-foot metal water tower.

It was a midwestern winter day, and a strong wind was blowing. Sheets thought the climb would not be too difficult, though, since the ladder that snaked up the side had a slight tilt and railings; he neglected to note that the last section of the climb would be up a narrow vertical arrangement of rungs, and that the top of the water tower was not flat but, rather, slightly pointed.

Father Joyce, an assistant administrator of Notre Dame, insisted on accompanying Sheets up the tower. Sheets demurred, pointing out to the priest that his elegant robe and tricornered hat would be severely damaged by such an exertion. Joyce insisted, and after removing his hat, followed Sheets up the side of the tower.

University of Notre Dame Library Tower mural: A swirl of scholars envelop the feet of Christ.

Resolutely, the two men climbed higher and higher. After ascending the final icy rung, they found that they still could not see the ground, because of the tower's inclined top. So, very gingerly, they slid down on their stomachs toward the tower's edge. There, they saw that all the risk was worthwhile: the mural's values and lines carried beautifully.

Descending from this precarious observation post was a little more nerve-shattering than their ascent, but the men managed to reach the ground again; their clothes were smeared with soot and dirt, their hands and faces were icy, but they had seen that the design was a success.

Sheets had a good feeling about this project. Its longevity was assured by the way the mosaic was put together, the colors were true, and the concept had held from idea to reality. "I think it actually does work as a mural in relation to architecture. The reflecting pool at the base of the tower gives it an extra dimension, and the colors are harmonious. The striking simplicity of working in such a telling, uncompromising medium demands some very hard and final decisions. The challenge was most stimulating, and I was pleased and excited to undertake it."

When Sheets undertook to create a dome mosaic for the National Shrine of the Immaculate Conception in Washington, D.C., in 1968, he was faced once again with problems of geometry and great size. In explaining the way in which he finally approached these, he uses the apt analogy of peeling an orange. "When an orange is peeled, and the sections pulled open, they are not straight lines. There has to be a bow in each edge so that the sections fit the rounded form. With this in mind, and after many attempts, I finally worked out a bowed form analogous to the

dome." The specifications had to be exact, as the dome was fabricated in Germany and shipped back to the United States for installation.

The mosaic's brilliant colors shimmer one hundred feet above the shrine's floor. The design that Sheets created centers around the apocalypse: the Lamb of God is in the center, intersected in cross formation by the great saints of the Church. Between the major figures are symbolic representations important in Catholic dogma. The aura of the Lamb is powerful, and Sheets credits it as one of the best things he and his group did.

Sheets also designed the mural that stretches across a side wall panel and the smaller domes of the shrine's more intimate Lady Chapel. This mosaic is a melange of figures representing every race of mankind; the artist described it as "tender, yet bold," and indeed the effect complements the small side chapel beautifully.

Mosaics appeal strongly to Sheets—there is a finality and honesty about them that he treasures. Too, they are compatible with his preference for things that are strongly designed and not "fussy." "The minute you place one stone, one color, one texture, next to another, you've committed yourself to something that must stand on its own. I enjoy that quality."

While the demands of working in mosaic have often tested Sheets's ingenuity, few projects have posed such problems as the one he undertook in 1968 for the Hilton hotel group. They wanted a rainbow, fabricated from Interpace ceramic tiles, for a space that measured 27 feet wide and 280 feet high. The success with which Sheets met these requirements is viewed daily by thousands of travelers; as they fly toward Honolulu, a graceful, semiabstract arc seems to rise out of the ocean. The lush tropical hills and white sand

The powerful aura of the Lamb of God is translated into mosaic in this Sheets design for the dome of the National Shrine of the Immaculate Conception, Washington, D.C.

Towering above an island paradise, the Honolulu Hawaii Hilton rainbow mural illustrates an ingenious use of ceramic tile.

beaches reinforce the rainbow's promise of paradise.

The concept was quite simple, but the mechanics of its creation were exceedingly complex. As the rainbow was to be made from the 12-inch-square tiles, the most effective way to avoid harsh edges of color would have been to hand paint each individual tile. Cost prohibited that approach, however. Sheets solved the difficulty by hiring twenty-five talented art students to trace the design onto the tiles that had been laid out on the factory floor. Then, painters with spray guns were fitted with harnesses and suspended by wires, much like Mary Martin in *Peter Pan*. Dangling in mid-air, the men applied the glaze color from above, filling in the spaces between the lines. After the coloring process was completed, each of the 204,000 tiles was numbered and fired.

As the company that had contracted to assemble the rainbow on the Honolulu Hilton's façade began its job, everyone watched intently. To their pleasure, the rainbow arose flawlessly, its colors glowing. Sheets credits the student assistants' diligence and enthusiasm with much of this tile mural's success.

Many hands and skills were needed to complete these large projects, but there were others that Sheets worked on essentially alone. One of them was for United Airlines, a commission that began in 1951 and spanned a decade. The initial contact with the airline came from Robert Johnson, who was then executive vice president of the company. Summoned to Chicago for a briefing on the proposed project, Sheets soon learned that United was offering him a traveler's dream come true. They wanted him to do thirteen original watercolor paintings each year; the subjects were to symbolize the major attractions of the company's many service areas. Naturally, the artist would fly

at no cost, and his expenses would be covered in addition to the stipend allotted for the work.

To Sheets, with his fascination for the unfamiliar and his zest for adventure, this must have seemed a divinely inspired opportunity. For nine of the next eleven years, he flew from resort to resort, executing 22-by-30-inch watercolor paintings. United required only that the works be representations of the areas; Sheets was able to endow each with all the painterly qualities he desired.

Ultimately, each year's output was transformed into beautifully reproduced promotional calendar illustrations. People were also given the opportunity to purchase, for a nominal sum, full-size color reproductions of any of the paintings included in the calendars.

This commission provided Sheets with many rewarding opportunities to paint areas of rare beauty; it also was the occasion for some memorable experiences, as happened one winter when he was asked to paint the Sun Valley, Idaho, ski resort.

At the time, Sheets and his family were living in Hawaii. With very little notice before departing for the mainland, Sheets quickly threw some clothes together, assembled his painting materials, and boarded the United Airlines' flight for his destination. Sheets had been in Hawaii for quite some time, and as a result, his wardrobe was geared for the tropical climate. Not long after his arrival in the ski area he discovered that the clothes he had brought with him would not be adequate. He found that the "Sun" in "Sun Valley" did not provide as much warmth as the name implied.

Resolute, and determined to finish his assignment, he took his materials and went up on the chair lift so he could get a good, panoramic view of the area. His paints promptly froze, as did his hands and feet; his camera, which he brought so he could have photos for reference, also froze.

Part way up the mountain, he stumbled off the lift and staggered to the small gate house, where a surly, fire-warmed attendant would not allow him to enter, but did direct him to a sign pointing west. If he followed that direction for about five hundred feet, Sheets was told, he would find a route back to the lodge.

Leaving his paints behind, he walked over a hard crust of snow toward the point indicated. Trudging along in his street shoes, it soon became apparent to him that the wisdom of the whole idea of returning to the lodge on foot was doubtful. About a hundred and fifty feet from the shed, his next step went into soft snow and he found himself sunk up to his shoulders below the surface. He moved an arm and descended another foot into the snow; now, only his head was above the surface.

Sheets had a moment of panic, followed by despair, as this area was not commonly popular with skiers. As the minutes passed, he began to wonder if he was destined to remain immobilized forever. His musings turned to a mixture of terror and hope when he saw, flashing over the snow directly at his head, two skiers. Frantically, he began to shout for help. It must have startled the men to see an apparently disembodied head at ground level; they came to a stop in a spray of powder and howled with laughter. Sheets, meanwhile, carefully worked his arms free and extended them above the surface. When they had themselves under control, each skier took an arm and, in corkscrew fashion, twirled the artist up out of the hole and helped him back onto solid snow. As they

sped off down the mountain, Sheets could hear their laughter ringing in the brittle air.

The artist struggled back to the gate house, burst in, and angrily berated the attendant for sending him off into that near-fatal area. The attendant replied that as the snow was only ninety feet deep at that point, he would have been found in the spring. Shivering, angry, and frustrated, Sheets struggled back onto the lift with his gear and took the return chair lift back down to the roaring fire of the lodge, where he thawed out and recaptured from memory the sight of Sun Valley from the ski lift.

The original watercolor paintings—117 in all—are still maintained as a permanent collection by United Airlines at their corporate headquarters in Chicago, Illinois.

In true teaching tradition, Sheets initiated his entrepreneurial enterprise, Millard Sheets Designs, Inc., trained others in the skills he had mastered, and gave them encouragement and the opportunity to produce. Functioning as the executive artist so many have called him, Sheets focused his organizational as well as creative abilities and proved time and again that artists have a productive, creative role to play. Financial considerations were, of course, important, as the funds he received for the studio's work enabled him both to continue producing beauty and to support himself, his family, and those who worked for him.

Money was not uppermost, however. The design studio was a medieval workshop revived, and the opportunity it offered for young artists to learn and develop their talents and reach out to others through their work was the propelling stimulus. Sheets firmly believes—and practices this belief—that art is not created in a vacuum, for oneself alone. Art has a purpose, a spirit that must be shared.

Sharing, teaching, leading, taking risks—Millard Sheets exemplifies the best of creative professionalism, and his many clients, students, and associates value him for it.

OLD COLONIAL HOUSE OF RANGAROA   *watercolor   22 x 30 inches   1980*

CONCLUSION

Havelock Ellis, that astute voyager in the human psyche, once observed that art is its creator's autobiography. Hartley Burr Alexander, the philosopher Sheets respected so much, was stunned by his first exposure to van Gogh's work—he felt that he had seen the essence of the artist's tormented life in van Gogh's paintings. Millard Sheets's life is also chronicled by the work he has produced, particularly his paintings. His childhood in golden California, the horrors of World War II in India, his fascination with foreign cultures, the depth of his concern for the form that is the underpinning of all life—these are readily visible, captured on canvas or paper for posterity. The abstractions of Sheets's personal experiences are made concrete during a career that stretches over six decades and a multitude of disciplines.

Quantifying this career—reducing it to mere numbers and categories—is possible, although in many cases the results are staggering: approximately 4,000 paintings completed, 47 workshops conducted, 52 years of teaching, 49 art jury positions, 70 buildings designed and executed, and so on. These statistics, however amazing, do not speak to the more vital question: How does one sum up the life and contribution of a man who has been so prolific in so many areas?

An elegant sense of continuity runs throughout Sheets's life and art. Beginning in childhood, a responsive evolution enabled him to stretch toward the next rung on the ladder of experience.

From his early murals, executed while he was still learning techniques from Tolles Chamberlain, to the paintings of Mexico that he completed after his 1983 workshop there, and all the work in between, Sheets's reach has rarely exceeded his grasp. He practiced what he learned, then he refined and expanded these skills and talents in ever-widening circles. His classes in architectural rendering led to his meeting with Cass Gilbert, who in turn directed his attention to architectural design. The ultimate result of this exploration was, of course, the landmark production of buildings that both utilized art as core components and were works of art themselves—Home Savings and the Masonic temples in Los Angeles and San Francisco.

Millard Sheets's far-reaching vision has enabled him to articulate the opportunities that have come his way, and his spirit and energy have helped those opportunities happen. For, underneath all of Millard Sheets's talent and vision is an absolutely indomitable will, a force that has driven him forward and spurred him to great heights of achievement within his artistic and creative sphere.

Gracious, thoughtful, and generous, Sheets gives freely of his time and experience. He laughs easily and is open and responsive to new ideas and concepts. His positive attitude generates an equally affirmative response in those whom he touches. As Frank Watrous, noted furniture designer, has commented: "There's something about Millard. He makes you think you can do things you thought you couldn't—before you know what's happening, you're actually *doing* them. I've lived off Millard Sheets's enthusiasm for twenty years."

The capacity to inspire this type of response is surely a gift that few possess, but one that Sheets has had since his earliest days as a student at Chouinard's. His amiability and charm reinforce his ability to move people in directions in which they have hesitated to go. Even more fundamental to his personality, though, is his determination. Sheets knows exactly what he wants to achieve and takes steps necessary to do so. This characteristic has sometimes presented itself as authoritarian, and Sheets's dislike of being controverted is evident. Combined with his insight and zest for accomplishment, however, these features of his personality take on a positive aspect.

Giving people responsibility and then expecting the best from them has almost always been effective for Sheets, and it is this willingness to grant the veracity and competency of others that is one of his most attractive assets. Sheets exudes a glow of vitality, even into his seventies, a glow that draws and inspires those who come into contact with him. Above all, he has the courage of his convictions, and he does not hesitate to express them. Sheets may delight, offend, entertain, or move to anger those who listen, but he never fails to charm.

Whatever it is, in art or anything else, it's who you are that determines what you produce. How deeply you love is critical to the end result of any effort. My chief quarrel with many educators is that they become primarily involved with technique and style but avoid substance. By substance, I don't mean just the technical skill to produce a painting or sculpture, although that is, of course, very important. An artist also has to involve his mind and his heart. In America, skills are way out in front—theories of "what makes a painting." But if the artist has nothing to say, what is the benefit? Art cannot be created from art. Talent isn't enough; without the quality of mind and spirit and the desire to express something close to your heart, talent is merely a facile gift.

Facileness is an anathema to Sheets, as is creativity directed too often at financial gain. "Artists must recognize that they have a great responsibility. They must build bridges between beauty and function. If they are financially enriched in the process, that is good. But it cannot be the sole motivation. If it is, society is doomed to pedestrian design, and aesthetically oppressive surroundings."

Millard Sheets lives by the precepts he espouses. He is a fighter, struggling to make people see that form and function are not antithetical but complementary concepts. In his fusion of art and architecture, with his hearty evangelizing for a more international attitude toward art and environment, Sheets has been both a practical and a philosophical influence. He has struggled with bureaucrats and red tape, questioned conventional wisdom, done battle with highly placed members of business and social groups. On occasion, he has even opposed the seemingly sacrosanct judgment of art critics. The results of all this activity have been, for the most part, positive; he feels he has helped advance good, workable solutions to problems of design, organization, and focus in a socially responsible fashion.

Sheets's efforts in these realms have often taken time away from his personal artistic endeavors. "Maybe I've gone off in too many directions, tried to do too much. Maybe I ought to have stayed with my paintings—only that." It is difficult to accept that he really believes this, however; Sheets seems to have required numerous outlets for his creative energy and may well have become embittered and frustrated if he had followed his own speculation.

Sharing, giving, working, thinking—Millard Sheets has indeed lived a most "outrageously enjoyable life," multidimensional and as rich as any of his tapestries, mosaics, or paintings. The effects of his art, personality, philosophy, and teaching spread in ever-widening ripples as those who he has touched modify and expand his ideas to fit special needs. Without a doubt, Millard Sheets's immortality is ensured—the legacy of his personality and philosophy is as important as his artistic accomplishments.

MILLARD SHEETS

· RETROSPECTIVE ·

The outstanding qualities of Sheets's art are its joyful and buoyant response to the picturesque aspects of California that appeal to him . . . an ever-present faculty that sometimes makes a picture out of the slightest elements with what would seem to be a native talent . . . beautiful, luminous color already gives distinction to his pictures.

ARTHUR MILLIER
Los Angeles Times

ROYAL CAMP   *oil   32 x 36 inches   1928*

ROCKS OF PALOS VERDES   *oil   32 x 36 inches   1929*

SPRING STREET, L.A.   *oil   32 x 36 inches   1930*

OLD MILL, BIG SUR *watercolor 22 x 30 inches 1933*

In the summer of 1933, in the course of a six-week painting class, Millard Sheets changed my life. . . . His extraordinary spirit, talent, and persuasiveness have been put in service of a philosophy which in itself has been widely inspiring . . . hundreds of young artists, and dozens of communities have been affected by his vision of the arts as integral to the fabric of life.

DAVID W. SCOTT
National Gallery of Art
Washington, D.C.

BLACK HORSE   *watercolor   14¹/₂ x 22 inches   1934*

TENEMENT FLATS   *oil   40 x 50 inches   1934*

HOG LOT *watercolor* $15^{3}/_{8}$ x $22^{7}/_{8}$ *inches* *ca. 1934*

MYSTIC NIGHT
watercolor   30 x 22 inches   1937

HORSES OF PADUA   *watercolor*   *22 x 29⅝ inches   1939*

Without Millard Sheets's energy and direction [I believe] that it is questionable whether there would ever have been a . . . California School.

E. GENE CRAIN

BRINGING OUT THE STALLION *oil   40 x 50 inches   1940*

FAMINE, INDIA — MOTHER AND CHILD
watercolor   30 x 40 inches   1943

KARACHI POULTRYMAN
oil   32 x 40 inches   1944

DEAD TANK CAPTAIN, BURMA *watercolor* 35½ x 49½ *inches* *1944*

BOMBED CRUCIFIX
oil   30 x 40 inches   1946

As a man of many talents, Millard Sheets has influenced the art world for over sixty years. By incorporating good design, a love of life, and a thorough understanding of art history, his artistic efforts have contributed significantly to American society.

WILLIAM G. OTTON
Director
Laguna Beach Museum of Art

ANNABELLA
oil   30 x 48 inches   1947

SUNDAY MORNING, KONA *watercolor 22 x 30 inches 1951*

MINNESOTA RIVER   *watercolor   22 x 30 inches   1952*

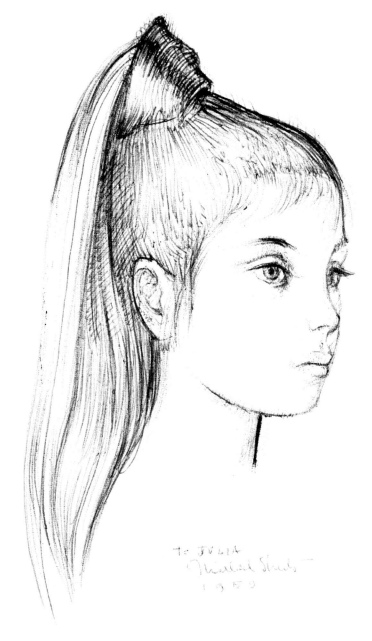

JULIA *sketch* 1959

[As a young man,] Millard Sheets was a fresh, new personality who won prizes and had shows. He built the momentum which made people look to California.

PHIL DIKE

TURKISH WOMEN *sketch* 1959

AFRICA *sketch* 1962

BÜRGENSTOCK, SWITZERLAND *sketch* 1964

DEEP WOODS
acrylic   29½ x 21½ inches   1966

RICE PADDIES, NEPAL   *watercolor   22 x 30 inches   1967*

Millard Sheets is deeply committed to the ideal of sharing one's talents, and he inspires his fellow artists to serve society with their aesthetic awareness. Artists, he believes, have the insight to positively affect our environment. A man of visionary mind and generous spirit, Sheets is a living example of his own creed.

MARY CARROLL NELSON

GROUNDED RAINBOWS   *watercolor   22 x 30 inches   1968*

UNITED STATES *sketch* 1970

TAHITI *sketch* 1972

FRUIT AND A NEW GUINEA BOWL   *watercolor   22 x 30 inches   1977*

TWO FRIENDS OF MOOREA *acrylic   29 x 40 inches   1978*

TAHITI *sketch* 1966

WOMEN OF THE FIELDS, YUGOSLAVIA   *watercolor*   *22 x 33 inches*   *1978*

He is a reflective and articulate artist, someone truly adjusted to his world and able to find in it an inexhaustible font of inspiration for his creative energies. An abiding optimism that characterizes whatever he does is reflected in the lyrical quality of his paintings. Their rhythmic configurations, vibrant colors, and harmonious designs converge into clearly defined images of glowing appeal.

LAWRENCE A. FLEISHMAN
Director, Kennedy Galleries
New York City

AMISH BARNS, PENNSYLVANIA   *watercolor*   *22 x 30 inches*   *1979*

SPRING IN DEEP WOOD, CALIFORNIA   *watercolor   21 x 29 inches   1979*

THE EDGE OF THE MOPTI MARKET, AFRICA   *watercolor   22 x 30 inches   1979*

ROSEMARY IN GREEN AND RED
acrylic 40 x 29 inches 1980

ON THE EDGE OF COOK BAY, MOOREA *watercolor 22 x 30 inches 1980*

[Sheets] is a superb draftsman, a subtle yet daring and opulent colorist, and a romantic . . . weaving intricate patterns with rhythmic, arresting, and vital figures.

EMILY GENAUER
New York *World-Telegram*

SAMPANS, HONG KONG *watercolor* *22 x 30 inches* *1981*

HONG KONG *sketch* *1961*

A BACK ROAD TO PATZCUARO, MEXICO   *watercolor   22 x 30 inches   1981*

CHILDREN AND PIGEONS IN THE PARK *watercolor 21 x 29 inches 1981*

ST. BASIL'S, MOSCOW, RUSSIA   *watercolor   30 x 40 inches   1982*

ARIZONA CORRAL   *watercolor   30 x 40 inches   1982*

BIRDS AND ROCKS BELOW STEWART'S POINT, CALIFORNIA   *watercolor   22 x 30 inches   1982*

Millard Sheets had star quality from the beginning . . . picture-making
[and] design were almost as natural to him as breathing. He wrote his
paintings with a brush.

PHIL PARADISE

INDIAN CHURCH, NEW MEXICO *watercolor 22 x 30 inches 1982*

MENDOCINO COAST   *watercolor   22 x 30 inches   1983*

SPRING PLOUGHING, MEXICO *watercolor   22 x 30 inches   1983*

WATERMELON LADY *watercolor 22 x 30 inches 1983*

To become an artist, one must become a total person. The broader the base of general education, the more able the artist is to cope with the environment. I believe, too, that gratitude for life itself is basic to the development of insight beyond the average.

MILLARD SHEETS

ACKNOWLEDGMENTS

IN ASSEMBLING THE MATERIAL FOR THIS BOOK, I had the generous help of my many artist-friends—Phil Dike, Rex and Joan Brandt, Phil Paradise, among others—as well as a great many individuals who were kind enough to share their observations and memories of Millard Sheets with me: his sons, Owen, David, and John, daughter Carolyn, Carolyn Ahmanson, Richard Armour, Frances Commons, Gould Eddy, Ruth Hatfield, Elizabeth Hopkins, Beth Baskerville McNaughton, Sarah Millier, Joseph Mugnaini, and Charles Shelton. Finally, I would be remiss if I did not thank Millard and Mary Sheets, whose unstinting patience and thoughtfulness helped bring this book to completion.

The University of California at Los Angeles has compiled thirty oral history interviews with a variety of artists, collectors, curators, and dealers; this material has been made freely available to authors and researchers. The two-volume set entitled *Los Angeles Art Community: Millard Sheets* was a valuable resource not only for the verification of specific details, such as dates and names, but also for the insights elicited by interviewer George Goodwin's questions. This comprehensive series of edited and bound interviews was most helpful.

CHRONOLOGY

1907   Born June 24, Pomona, California to Milly Owen and John Gaspar Sheets

1925   Graduated, Pomona High School

1927–29   Taught watercolor painting, Chouinard School of Art, Los Angeles, California

1929   Graduated, Chouinard School of Art, Los Angeles, California

European trip

1930   Painting, *Women of Cartagena,* accepted by jury of Carnegie International Exhibition, Pittsburgh, Pennsylvania

1932   Appointed Head of Art Department, Scripps College, Claremont, California

1935   *Millard Sheets,* by Merle Armitage, published

1936   Designer, Houbigant displays

1936–55   Director, Scripps College Art Department

1939–40   Designer, seventeen air schools for United States Air Force

1940–42   Taught regional painting workshops, New Mexico and Texas

1940–56   Director of Art Exhibition, Los Angeles County Fair, Pomona, California

1941   Lecturer, Association of American Universities (also 1943)

1943–44   Artist-correspondent for *Life* magazine; covered World War II, China-Burma-India front

1953   Designer, supervisor of construction for National American Insurance Company building, Los Angeles, California

1953–59   Director, Los Angeles County Art Institute (Otis-Parson's Art Institute)

1954   Designer, Ahmanson Bank and Trust Company, Los Angeles, California

1954–75   Designer, forty Home Savings and Loan buildings

1955–72   Balch Lectureship, Scripps College, Claremont, California

1956   Illustrated *The Beach of Falesa,* by Robert Louis Stevenson, for the Limited Editions Club, New York

1958   Commissioned by United States Air Force to visit Formosa

1959   Purchased property on Mendocino coast

Guest of the West German government

1960   Barking Rocks completed

1960–61   Participant, American Specialist Program, United States Department of State; visited and lectured in Turkey and USSR

1963–83 Taught Hewitt Brothers Painting Workshops; twenty-two, world-wide

1964–73 Director of Design, Interpace Corporation (formerly Gladding-McBean)

1965 Illustrated *The Nigger of the Narcissus,* by Joseph Conrad

1967–75 Member of the Board of Directors, California Institute of the Arts (Cal Arts)

1976 Taught Jade Fon Painting Workshops, Asilomar, California (also 1977, 1981)

1976–83 Taught regional painting workshops: California, Arizona, New Mexico, Utah, Texas, Virginia, Hawaii

1976 Participant, University of California at Los Angeles oral history project: "Los Angeles Art Community"

1979 Visited West Africa

1980 Illustrated *West African Journal,* written by Mary Baskerville Sheets

1983 Produced *Your Drawing is a Measure of Your Mind*

MURALS AND MOSAICS

1929 Pasadena, California, Young Men's Christian Association

1930 Los Angeles, California, State Mutual Building

1931 Los Angeles, California, J. W. Robinson Company

1932 Los Angeles, California, Bullocks Men's Stores
South Pasadena Junior High School: frescoes

1938 San Francisco, California, San Francisco World Exposition: painted murals totaling 10,000 square feet

1946 Washington, D.C., Department of the Interior: mural entitled *Negro Education in America*

1953 Los Angeles, California, Church of the Precious Blood
Rochester, Minnesota, Mayo Clinic: painted mural entitled *Discovery–Invention–Experimentation*
Ventura, California, Our Lady of the Assumption Catholic Church

1954–75 California, 40 Home Savings and Loan buildings: 45 painted murals, 38 mosaic panels

1954 Pomona, California, Pomona First Federal Savings and Loan: painted mural entitled *History of Pomona*

1955 Dallas, Texas, Mercantile Bank
Dallas, Texas, Mercantile Continental Building: sculpture and mosaic mural

1957 Sacramento, California, American Trust Bank

1958 Palm Springs, California, Palm Springs Restaurant
San Antonio, Texas, Travis Savings and Loan: painted mural entitled *Death of Travis*

1959 Beverly Hills, California, Ahmanson Bank
Van Nuys, California, Van Nuys Savings and Loan

1960 Los Angeles, California, Scottish Rite Temple: exterior and interior mosaics and murals and painted lobby mural entitled *History of Masonry in California*
Lubbock, Texas, Lubbock National Bank
Lubbock, Texas, Southwest Bank of Lubbock

1962 Detroit, Michigan, Detroit Public Library: exterior façade
Pomona, California, Pomona Mall

1964 Claremont, California, Pomona First Federal Savings and Loan
Houston, Texas, Houston Savings and Loan
South Bend, Indiana, University of Notre Dame: mural for Library Tower façade

1965 San Francisco, California, Scottish Rite Temple

1966 Novato, California, Great Western Savings and Loan

1968 Honolulu, Hawaii, Honolulu Hilton: exterior façade, ceramic tile mural, *Rainbow*
Washington, D.C., National Shrine of the Immaculate Conception: design for mosaic Dome of the Blessed Sacrament

1970 Tyler, Texas, bank and country club
Washington, D.C., National Shrine of the Immaculate Conception: mosaic for dome and wall of Lady Chapel

1972 Los Angeles, California, Los Angeles City Hall East: two painted tile murals entitled *The Culture Brought to Los Angeles by the Races of the World*

1973   Claremont, California, The Garrison Theater:
            granite mosaic
        Menlo Park, California, *Sunset Magazine* head-
            quarters
1974   Beverly Hills, California, Beverly Wilshire Hotel
        Lubbock, Texas, Methodist Hospital, Charles
            Maedgen Memorial Room
        Ventura, California, Ventura Community Hos-
            pital: mosaic in collaboration with Susan Her-
            tel entitled *Nature Through the Eyes of Children*
1977   San Jose, California, San Jose Airport Terminal

SELECTED GROUP
AND ONE-MAN SHOWS

1929   Newhouse Galleries, Los Angeles, California
        Salon d'Automne, Paris, France
1930   Carnegie International Watercolor Exhibition,
            Pittsburgh, Pennsylvania (annually until
            World War II)
        Dalzell Hatfield Galleries (formerly Newhouse
            Galleries), Los Angeles, California (annual
            exhibitions through 1975)
        Los Angeles Museum of Art, Los Angeles,
            California
        San Diego Museum of Fine Arts, San Diego,
            California
1930–34 Art Institute of Chicago, Chicago, Illinois,
            International Watercolor Show
1931   Brooks Memorial Gallery, Memphis, Tennessee
        California Palace of the Legion of Honor, San
            Francisco, California
        Isaac Delgado Museum, New Orleans, Louisiana
        Kansas City Art Institute, Kansas City, Missouri
        Milwaukee Institute of Arts, Milwaukee,
            Wisconsin
        Museum of Fine Arts, Houston, Texas
        Pennsylvania Academy of Fine Arts,
            Philadelphia, Pennsylvania
        Philadelphia Watercolor Show, Philadelphia,
            Pennsylvania
        St. Louis Museum of Art, St. Louis, Missouri
        Witte Memorial Gallery, San Antonio, Texas
1932   Albany Museum of History and Art,
            Albany, New York

Baltimore Museum of Art, Baltimore, Maryland
Berkeley Museum of Art, Berkeley, California
Corcoran Gallery of Art, Washington, D.C.
High Museum of Art, Atlanta, Georgia
Los Angeles County Museum of Art,
    Los Angeles, California: *Angel's Flight*
Palace of Arts, Tucson, Arizona
University of Kansas School of Fine Arts,
    Lawrence, Kansas
University of Oklahoma School of Fine Arts,
    Norman, Oklahoma
University of Southern California, Los Angeles,
    California
1932–34 Century of Progress Exhibition, Chicago,
    Illinois
1934   All-California Art Exhibition: *Abandoned*
        Honolulu Academy of Fine Arts, Honolulu,
            Hawaii
        Milch Galleries, New York, New York
        Whitney Museum of American Art, New York,
            New York
1935   California Palace of the Legion of Honor,
            All-American Exhibition, San Francisco,
            California
        Toledo Museum of Art, Toledo, Ohio
1937   Courvoisier Gallery, San Francisco, California
        John Herron Art Institute, Minneapolis,
            Minnesota
1938   Art Institute of Chicago, Chicago, Illinois,
            International Watercolor Exhibition, Guest
            of Honor
1939   Baltimore Museum of Art, Baltimore,
            Maryland, "Six Living American Painters"
        Golden Gate International Exposition,
            San Francisco, California: *Alcatraz*
1941   *La Pintura Contemporánea Norte Americana,* Mexico
            City, Mexico; Bogotá, Colombia; Quito,
            Ecuador; Lima, Peru; Santiago, Chile; Caracas,
            Venezuela; Rio de Janeiro, Brazil; Montevideo,
            Uruguay; Buenos Aires, Argentina
1944   Albany Institute of History and Art, Albany,
            New York, "American Drawing Annual:
            Drawing by Men and Women of the
            Armed Forces"

1945 Denver Art Museum, Denver, Colorado
1950 Pasadena Art Institute, Pasadena, California, "Millard Sheets in Retrospect, 1929–1950"
1954 Arizona State College Collection of American Art, Tempe, Arizona: *Mazatlan Woman*
1955 Artists of the United States in Latin America, Pan-American Union, Washington, D.C.: *Hills of Patzcuaro, Mexico*
Third Biennial of San Paulo (United States Representation), Rio de Janeiro, Brazil: *Lonely Harbor*
1958 Tweed Gallery, University of Minnesota, Duluth, Minnesota
1964 Arthur Tooth Galleries, London, England
1966 Metropolitan Museum of Art, New York, New York, "Centennial Exhibition of American Watercolor Society": *Goats of Guaymas*
1972 Phoenix Art Museum, Phoenix, Arizona, "Today's Artist and the West": *Ancient Cottonwood, New Mexico*
1974 Laguna Beach Museum of Art, Laguna Beach, California, "California National Watercolor Show"
1976 Bohemian Club, San Francisco, California
San Francisco Museum of Modern Art, San Francisco, California, "Modern California Painters": *Angel's Flight*
Scripps College, Claremont, California, "Retrospective—Millard Sheets"
1978 Fresno Art Center, Fresno, California, "Southern California School of Watercolor, 1928 to 1978"
Kennedy Galleries, New York, New York (also in 1980, 1982)
1979 Laguna Beach Museum of Art, Laguna Beach, California, "Southern California Artists, 1890–1940": *The White Barn*
1980 Los Angeles Museum of Art, Los Angeles, California, "Painting and Sculpture in Los Angeles, 1900–1945": *Angel's Flight*
Union League Club, New York, New York, "American Watercolor Painting Since the Mid-19th Century"

1981 Newport Harbor Art Museum and Santa Barbara Museum of Art, California, "California, The State of Landscape, 1872–1981"
Santa Fe East, Santa Fe, New Mexico
1982 Walla Walla College Department of Art, Walla Walla, Washington
1983 Crocker Art Museum Association, Sacramento, California, "Sacramento Collects"
Laguna Beach Museum of Art, Laguna Beach, California
National Museum of American Art, Smithsonian Institution, Washington, D.C., "Social Concern and Urban Realism, American Painting of the Thirties" Traveling Exhibition: *Tenement Flats*
Sangre de Cristo Art Center, Pueblo, Colorado
Texas Tech Museum of Art, Lubbock, Texas, "Millard Sheets—Retrospective"
1984 Monterey Peninsula Museum of Art, "Millard Sheets—Retrospective"

SELECTED HONORS AND AWARDS

1922 California Watercolor Society, Second Prize
1925 Los Angeles County Fair, First Prize, Oil: *Painters and Scrapers*
1928 Arizona State Fair, Phoenix, First Landscape Purchase Prize
1929 Witte Museum, San Antonio, Texas, Edward B. Davis competition, Second Prize: *The Goat Ranch*
1932 Los Angeles County Museum of Art, Painting Prize: *Angel's Flight*
1938 Art Institute of Chicago, Watson F. Blair Purchase Prize: *Mystic Night*
Carnegie International Watercolor Exhibition, Guest of Honor
1939 Philadelphia Watercolor Club Prize
1943 Pennsylvania Academy of Fine Arts, Dana Watercolor Medal
1946 Los Angeles County Museum of Art, Drawing Prize
National Watercolor Society, President
United States Department of War, Citation for Outstanding and Conspicuous Service as Accredited War Correspondent
1951 Artists Guild of Chicago, Gold Brush Award

1955 Audubon Artists, Honorary Member
1962 Otis Art Institute, Master of Fine Arts
1964 American Institute of Building Design, Award
      for Contribution to the Improvement of the
      Designing Profession
      University of Notre Dame, South Bend, Indiana,
      Honorary Doctor of Laws Degree
1971 Ceramic Tile Institute, Decorator's Award
1977 National Watercolor Society, Citation in Recog-
      nition of Distinctive Achievements During Fifty
      Years of Membership, 1927–1977
1981 The Bicentennial of the City of Los Angeles, Certifi-
      cate of Achievement on the Occasion of Tribute to
      the Men and Women of Achievement

SELECTED PERMANENT COLLECTIONS

Albany Museum of History and Art, Albany, New York
Arizona State Fair Permanent Collection, Phoenix,
  Arizona
Art Institute of Chicago, Chicago, Illinois
Brooklyn Museum, Brooklyn, New York
Carnegie Institute, Pittsburgh, Pennsylvania
Cleveland Museum of Art, Cleveland, Ohio
M. H. de Young Memorial Museum, San Francisco,
  California
Fort Worth Museum Permanent Collection, Fort Worth,
  Texas
Frye Galleries, Seattle, Washington
Houston Museum of Art, Houston, Texas
Laguna Beach Museum of Art, Laguna Beach, California
Los Angeles County Museum of Art Permanent
  Collection, Los Angeles, California

Los Angeles Public Library Print Collection, Los Angeles,
  California
Metropolitan Museum of Art, New York, New York
Municipal Collection, Phoenix, Arizona
Museum of Modern Art, New York, New York
National Museum of American Art, Smithsonian
  Institution, Washington, D.C.
Rhode Island School of Design, Providence, Rhode Island
San Diego Museum Permanent Collection, San Diego,
  California
San Francisco Museum of Art, San Francisco, California
Seattle Art Museum, Seattle, Washington
United States Air Force, Washington, D.C.
United States Department of Defense, Paintings of War
  for *Life,* Washington, D.C.
Whitney Museum of American Art, New York,
  New York
Howard S. Wilson Memorial Collection, Lincoln,
  Nebraska
Witte Memorial Gallery, San Antonio, Texas

MEMBERSHIPS

Art Directors Guild
Bohemian Club
California Watercolor Society
Economic Round Table
National Academy of Design
National Watercolor Society
The Rancheros

ART INDEX

DESIGNED BY MICHAEL HOLLAR
COMPOSED IN PHOTOTYPE BEMBO
WITH DISPLAY LINES IN DELPHIAN AND BEMBO
PRINTED ON QUINTESSENCE DULL
AT THE PRESS IN THE PINES

NORTHLAND PRESS